Praise for

THE FIVE EMBODIMENTS

———————————

"As a leader and entrepreneur, I've seen what can happen when you put humanity first at work: Connection deepens. Trust grows. Relationships flourish. And your bottom line? Better than ever. But I learned about it the hard way. *The Five Embodiments* is the guide to human-focused leadership that I wish I'd had when I started my business. It's simple, accessible, and research-backed, and it will help leaders at all levels create cultures of connection and psychological safety. If you're looking to bring humanity back to your workplace but aren't sure where to start, start here."

—KRISTEN HADEED, CEO, author of *Permission to Screw Up: How I Learned to Lead by Doing (Almost) Everything Wrong*

"*The Five Embodiments* resonates with me on several levels. The way Matt and Jean connect the loneliness epidemic and the obstacles to making meaningful human connections at work is timely and on point. Work has a massive impact on our very being, and the framework this book offers is a novel solution to a widespread problem. When I was building businesses in the '80s, interpersonal human relationships were far more front and center, yet today the norm is much more transactional. The 'embodiments' are an innovative approach to building the skills that many of today's leaders lack. I love how they brought their ideas to life and wove in case studies, stories, and practical takeaways. This is not a system that any company I know of can look at and say 'We already do that.' Despite all the leadership training out there, no one is focusing on this. This is truly a different approach to leadership and in my opinion only has upside."

—STEVE PRUETT, Executive Chairman, Cox Media; author, *The Gain Principle*

"If you've ever whispered, 'There's gotta be a better way' into your coffee between meetings—this book offers it. *The Five Embodiments* is a guide and invitation to making leadership more relational, more intentional, and way more human. If you want to lead in a way that actually serves people and not just performance metrics, this one's for you. It will help you show up with greater clarity, compassion, and the courage to act."

—STEPHEN "SHED" SHEDLETZKY, speaker; coach; author, *Speak-Up Culture: When Leaders Truly Listen, People Step Up*

"Finally, a leadership book that doesn't just inspire. It equips. As someone leading sales, marketing, and culture for a large organization, I've read a lot of leadership books—but *The Five Embodiments* landed differently. The ideas aren't new, but the way they're framed—curiosity, authenticity, care, gratitude, and ownership—makes them feel accessible and actionable. This book gave me practical tools to grow and to bring my team along for the ride. The chapter wrap-ups and practice prompts made it easy to stay engaged—and easy to come back to. The consistency story from Jean (about yoga and learning to sway instead of staying rigid) hit me hard. Clear, actionable, and actually useful— this is the kind of leadership book you'll dog-ear and revisit again and again."

—CHAD ALLERS, Vice President of Sales and Marketing, Bargreen Ellingson

"Every leader who wants to move from feeling stuck to empowered will benefit from reading *The Five Embodiments*. Jean and Matt provide the perfect blend of story, statistics, and savvy to apply the concepts for real change. Society continues to shift, and these embodiments are no longer just a 'nice-to-have' for leaders. New generations are insisting on returning humanity to the workplace, whether they are virtual, hybrid, or full-time in old-fashioned in-person offices, so take the step in your growth journey by reading this book and embodying these life-changing concepts."

—DR. LAURA GALLAHER, speaker, author, and CEO at Gallaher Edge

"When it comes to truly human leadership, it's not about what we know how to do—it's about how we do it. This book lays out a clear, actionable path to lead with presence, purpose, and connection. It's a guide for showing up better—for your people and yourself."

—RICH DIVINEY, retired Navy SEAL commander and bestselling author of *The Attributes* and *Masters of Uncertainty*

"As a CEO of a growing team, I'm always seeking out thoughtful resources that support both personal growth and the development of effective, connected teams. *The Five Embodiments* is one of those books that truly stands out—a must-read for current and aspiring leaders who understand that leadership is ultimately about people, not just performance. This book presents a powerful framework rooted in human-focused leadership. It reinforces a critical truth: If you want vision to become reality, it must be built on the foundation of strong, genuine relationships. What I found especially impactful is how it shifts the traditional view of management. Instead of leaders seeing themselves as above their teams, *The Five Embodiments* positions leadership as something that happens *with* others, not *to* them. Every person plays a vital role, and success is shared—just like in a high-functioning credit union. One concept that really resonated with me is the broader perspective on relationships—not just the interaction between individuals, but the importance of intentionally nurturing the relationship itself. The book offers several insightful frameworks, such as the relationship triangle, the power of curiosity, the role of authenticity, and much more. These ideas are especially impactful in cooperative environments, where strong, intentional relationships are essential to achieving shared success. For anyone committed to growing as a leader—not just in title but through meaningful action and authentic connection—this book offers both challenge and inspiration. It encourages you to embrace a style of leadership that transforms teams and drives lasting success. Plus, the practical Quick Tips and reference materials included make it a valuable, hands-on resource you can put to work right away with your team."

—NATHAN CAPE, CEO, Minnequa Works Credit Union

THE FIVE EMBODIMENTS

A Guide to Human-Focused Leadership,
Stronger Relationships,
and a Workplace That Doesn't Suck

Jean Larkin | **Matt Dunsmoor**

amplify
an imprint of Amplify Publishing Group

amplify
an imprint of Amplify Publishing Group

www.amplifypublishinggroup.com

The Five Embodiments: A Guide to Human-Focused Leadership, Stronger Relationships, and a Workplace That Doesn't Suck

For permission or press requests, please contact: info@thefiveembodiments.com.

For more information, please contact:
Amplify Publishing, an imprint of Amplify Publishing Group
620 Herndon Parkway, Suite 220
Herndon, VA 20170
info@amplifypublishing.com

Library of Congress Control Number: 2025904503

CPSIA Code: PRV1025A

ISBN-13: 979-8-89138-357-9

Printed in the United States

To a future where work offers fulfillment to the majority, not just a select few. And for the human-focused leaders whose efforts bring connection to the world—this book is dedicated to you.

Contents

Introduction

"Oh shit, my toes are blue."

I looked down at my legs, bent underneath me on the bathroom floor, and then at my feet. I was having a bad reaction to the medicine my doctors had given me for pneumonia. I didn't even have the energy to react with appropriate shock or concern.

I called the doctor, stopped that round of medicine, went back to the hospital, got new medicine, and managed to get enough oxygen to return blood flow to my toes. When I got home, I climbed into bed and tried to fall asleep. After a few hours, I rolled over and noticed I had a text from my manager: "Hey, Jean, I know you're offline, but I need . . ."

* * *

I had sent a doctor's note prescribing a week of bed rest and didn't have it in me to do anything or help anyone. I couldn't even rest comfortably. Between the sickness and exhaustion, something that had been right there in front of me all along finally became clear: They didn't care about me; they only cared about what I did for them.

All the hours, the dedication, the sacrifices . . . that day I was the sickest I'd ever been in my life, and they still put their KPIs over my well-being.

I could never give them enough to satisfy their obsession with growth.

This story isn't unique. In fact, we have heard similar stories of overwork and burnout from every industry. While many people like to think it mostly happens at megacorporations, the reality couldn't be further from the truth. For decades, no matter the size of the organization, companies have looked at their employees as an expense rather than an asset. Bosses have forgotten that companies are not faceless, heartless entities. Every company is made of people: unique, complex human beings who have the power to make a huge impact.

And when companies focus on maximizing profits, they try to extract as much as possible from their people, even when sick, and often jump to layoffs after a bad quarter. This approach leads to a workplace environment where employees are disengaged, fearful, and consistently experiencing burnout, which, ironically, hurts a company's productivity, efficiency, and growth. More importantly, it bleeds into the personal and social lives of everyone at the company and affects their overall health and well-being.

We believe that the old paradigm is shifting, making way for something new.

We founded Octopy to help leaders and organizations become human focused.

To truly succeed in the coming decades, organizations need to let go of their singular focus on the bottom line and hold themselves to a higher standard. Human beings are wired for connection, so for an organization and its people to thrive, leaders must create a culture of connection and strong relationships. When we empower, trust, and take care of our people, they take care of the bottom line. And it starts with great leadership.

We believe in a life, including work, that gives people a sense of purpose and belonging. We believe that when leaders and company cultures become truly human focused, employees become better versions of themselves through work, not in spite of it. And we believe we can accomplish all of this while still improving bottom-line performance.

It begins with investing in our people—with our time, energy, and, yes, even money. When we invest in the right things, we create a system that's more equitable for everyone involved, not just those at the top. We create a system that is sustainable, meaningful, and fulfilling. And while changing the entire system may sound like a daunting task, it begins with a first step. When we spend our time and energy intentionally connecting with those around us, our influence and ability to shape the system grows.

With all this in mind, we're excited to share with you the five embodiments essential for human-focused leadership, stronger relationships, and creating workplaces that don't suck.

CHAPTER 1

A Loneliness Epidemic

Loneliness is proof that your innate search for connection is intact.
—**Martha Beck**

On May 2, 2023, the US surgeon general made a historic announcement. It wasn't about the dangers of vices like cigarettes or binge drinking. It wasn't about a communicable disease like AIDS or the ever-present challenge of obesity. Dr. Vivek Murthy's warning was about an epidemic very different in tone and tenor. It was about loneliness. Here's what he said:

> Being socially disconnected is bad, for both individual and societal health. Research shows that loneliness and isolation are associated with a greater risk of heart disease, dementia, stroke, depression, anxiety, and premature death. In fact, lacking connection can increase the risk of premature death to levels comparable to smoking daily. . . . Social connection is as fundamental to our mental and physical health as food, water, and sleep. And it affects our performance and productivity at work, school, and in our communities. Now is the time to invest in building social connection.[1]

Coming only a few years after the emergence of COVID-19, his words were unsurprising to most of us. After all, the global shutdown had isolated many of us from our friends and families. But even in the years leading up to the pandemic, roughly half of Americans reported experiencing loneliness.[2] Loneliness has been defined as "a discrepancy between a person's desired and actual social relationships."[3] Upon reviewing an array of research, what is clear is that experiencing loneliness is not about being alone but rather the sensation of lacking desired meaningful human connection.

What constitutes meaningful human connection? For some, it might mean seeing friends daily or gathering in large groups weekly; for others, it's about having one or two significant friendships and only monthly gatherings. Each individual's needs and preferences for the depth and breadth of relationships varies, but the baseline requirement for warm and meaningful connection is universally human.

In recent years a significant increase in depression, anxiety, and other mental health issues that our health system is woefully unprepared for has contributed to a national mental health crisis. As of April 2024, over 122 million people live in one of the 6,129 designated mental health care health professional shortage areas.[4]

Wherever you personally fall on the spectrum of loneliness plaguing our society, the current reality is that it's both a micro and a macro issue. It has profound effects on each of us individually, whether we personally feel disconnected and lonely or see changes in someone we love, or work with, due to lacking warm and meaningful connections. Societally, from the local to national and global scale, it influences political polarization, public health, policy preferences, trust in our neighbors, and how we interact with our communities both in person and online.

So, with public health, mental health, and physical health all on the line, it's imperative that we take action.

Human Beings Are Wired for Connection

For proof, we need not look further than our own biological design. Newborns are entirely dependent on caregivers for survival; they must form strong bonds, or attachments, to the adults who care for them. Accordingly, the feeling center of our brains develops first to facilitate those bonds. Throughout our development and into adulthood, our brains continue to release neurochemicals that reward connecting, being of service to others, and growing together.

Neuroscientists have demonstrated that feeling disconnection shares the very same neural pathways as physical pain.[5] The ache of loneliness is as real as the pain from a broken arm and needs just as much intention and effort to heal. Additionally, evidence shows that a lack of social connection can increase the risk of premature death as much as smoking up to fifteen cigarettes a day.[6]

The Harvard Study of Adult Development, which started in 1938, is the longest ongoing study of human happiness in modern history. Its researchers have collected data on thousands of human lives over eight decades. Here's how the current director, Dr. Robert Waldinger, described the study's main takeaway: "The people who turn out to be the happiest and the healthiest are those who have good, warm connections to others."[7]

The single best life choice you can make today is to invest in warm relationships, personally *and* professionally. We need to engage in relationships where we feel seen, heard, and valued—relationships that encourage us to participate authentically and reciprocate warmth. It really is that simple. As we've all learned, though, simple is not synonymous with easy, so this advice might be easier to hear than to implement. Nevertheless, we hope the insights in this book will help get you there.

With so much at stake, leaders in organizations can no longer expect employees to deal with "all of that emotional and relationship stuff" outside of work. But before we get into how to tackle these challenges, it's important that we first examine our context more fully so that we can better determine how to move forward.

How We Got Here

Although disappointed, we weren't shocked when Dr. Murthy published his report. After years of firsthand experience and reviewing Gallup's annual *State of the Global Workplace* report, we were aware of the consistently high levels of self-reported loneliness among workers. In fact, Gallup's 2025 report found that over a fifth of employees are lonely daily and that it is even higher for folks thirty-five and under.[8]

So, we set out to explore how we got here. What is unique about our current reality, or our lives until now, that contributes to loneliness? What societal structures exist to facilitate connection at pivotal times in our lives? Today loneliness affects the entire population, yet it disproportionately affects younger people—why?

SHRINKING THIRD PLACES

Although many recent discussions on loneliness start with the COVID-19 pandemic, there is a much longer history behind our loneliness epidemic. Urban sociologist Ray Oldenburg coined the term *third place* in reference to a familiar public spot or location that facilitates social interaction outside of where you live and work.[9] The probability of connecting with someone increases as you repeatedly run into them at a common place, be that a grocery store, a park, or a religious center. It isn't about what you do there, but the spaces themselves as a physical location to meet, get to know other people, and potentially develop relationships.

Major brands, such as Starbucks, have grown to global household names by positioning themselves as a third place. While cafés and private enterprises do offer one type of third place, there is an inherent exclusivity to being able to purchase something every time you desire social connection. Earlier generations enjoyed public third places, for example: public pools in communities were once widespread in the US. In the 1920s and 1930s, thousands of pools opened in the United States and drew in millions of swimmers. In 1950 there were only approximately 2,500 pools at private homes, and today that number is 10.3 million (which represents over 97 percent of all pools including private club, sports centers, schools, and municipal pools).[10] And although numbers are harder to find on the amount of municipal parks with recreation centers and free campsites with tables and grills (encouraging community members to come together and share a meal), one thing seems clear: Most communities have few or no free community spaces that serve as third places.

Robert D. Putnam, author of *Bowling Alone: The Collapse and Revival of American Community*, describes how a disintegration of social structures, including parent-teacher associations, clubs, and religious institutions, was well on its way by the end of the twentieth century.[11] Although the author originally researched the decades leading up to 1990 for his seminal 2000 book, the message still rings true in 2025, and Putnam continues his work today. In recent interviews, he shares how many core drivers of isolation have expanded and new ones continue to pop up, only exacerbating the problem in the time since he published his book. From commutes in separate vehicles to less time for community gatherings and televisions in everyone's homes, we have each experienced at least one of these drivers firsthand.

Putnam illustrates a pivotal shift with a pun that stuck with us: People began to stay home to watch *Friends* instead of going out to spend time with their friends.[12] In other words, communities of people who once spent much of their free time together at common third places connecting and socializing became increasingly isolated. Soon neighbors were more of a collection of individuals who spent their shrinking free time in private spaces, watching their own TV and swimming in their own pools rather than gathering as a community.

Beyond a decrease in municipal third spaces, the percentage of people congregating at religious and educational centers has also shifted.

FEWER CONGREGATION-BASED CONNECTIONS

At one point in history, most people in the US belonged to a church. Today, however, not even half of US adults are members of a mosque, synagogue, or church. In 1937, US church membership was 73 percent; by 2020, it fell to 47 percent (see graph, page 7).[13] Furthermore, those who are still members are less likely to regularly attend religious services than in decades past: Only 21 percent of US adults reported attending weekly services between 2021 and 2023.[14]

While, yes, there is a generational component, with fewer young adults in attendance, the decrease is seen across every generation, with the Traditionalist Generation (those born before 1946) seeing an 11 percent drop in church membership between 1998 and 2000 alone.

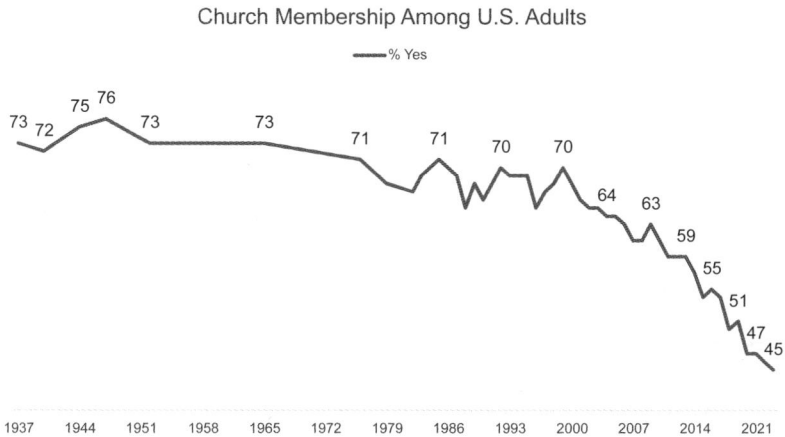

Church Membership Among U.S. Adults

—— % Yes

73 72 75 76 73 73 71 71 70 70 64 63 59 55 51 47 45

1937 1944 1951 1958 1965 1972 1979 1986 1993 2000 2007 2014 2021

To be clear—when we talk about third places, we're talking about *places*, not *activities*. Religion itself has a complicated relationship to loneliness. While some reports find certain religious people are less lonely, a recent review of the research found a significant positive correlation between religious affiliation and increased instances of loneliness.[15]

These diverging and seemingly contradictory results point to specific factors beyond religious affiliation or church membership as the core influences on a person's emotional health and loneliness. What we do know is having a familiar communal place that offers a no-to-low-cost option to gather as a community, connect, and even host events provides an opportunity to prevent loneliness.

The physical locations of religious centers historically have been home to many events with no religious affiliation, a space to invite friends and family from within and outside of the religious congregation to a single gathering place. Shrinking congregations means today, far fewer people belong to a center where they regularly see others, gather as a community, and host events.

SHIFTING SCHOOL-BASED CONNECTIONS

For many adults in previous generations, schools were a key third place. More than just a spot to drop off their kids, schools were a community hub where adults could meet, connect, and build relationships.

In 2006, it wasn't unusual for a grandparent to walk into a school to deliver a forgotten lunch or pop in to see the artwork in the halls if they missed the art show. It was common for younger and older community members alike to volunteer to support tutoring programs, extracurricular activities, arts programming, and sporting events.

In 2024 more households are made up of parents employed outside the home, and fewer parents have time to join the PTA or be a classroom parent. Additionally, younger generations have fewer children, if any at all. In 1976, 40 percent of forty- to forty-four-year-old moms had four or more children, but since the 1990s that same percentage has only two children.[16] Children and their activities introduce parents to more adults, but with fewer adults having many (or any) children, there is a growing percentage of the population who miss out on those opportunities to connect and build community.

Additionally, due to various influences, such as a drastic increase in gun violence in US schools, more schools are closed to their communities. So today, far fewer adults, whether recent grads, family members, or local volunteers, are regularly involved with school activities, making it less common to meet and connect with other adults.

THE INTERNET 2.0

An ever-increasing number of us have a hard time remembering the world before the existence of platforms like Myspace, Facebook, and Instagram—and before you ask, yes, the authors do remember Myspace; we are *that* old. Companies sold these platforms to us with the promise of increasing the ease and depth of connecting. And while some may argue that they succeeded in increasing the ease of connecting, we could also argue that they missed the mark on deepening relationships.

Social media followership is often a one-sided conversation. While we use terms like *connection* or *friend*, very little authentic connection exists, and among our social media contacts, we may have very few true friends. In an interview with Brené Brown, Esther Perel described this as "artificial intimacy" when one feels "I have a thousand friends, but not a single person to feed my cat."[17]

Especially in recent years, it has become clear through documentaries such as Netflix's *The Social Dilemma* that creating true connection among users is not a primary, secondary, or even tertiary goal of most social media platforms. The goal is content engagement and ad sales, and these companies have figured out how to trick our very biology into coming back for short bursts of dopamine. We smile, like, comment, and share, but the feelings aren't the same as being with one another and experiencing milestones and joyous moments together.

The Harvard Adult Development study found that the physical presence of a warm connection helps reduce the negative physiological effects of stress. Coming home to a warm connection can help us let go of our bad day, and that daily release is key to preventing burnout. Unfortunately, we don't all have a warm connection to come home to. And even for those of us who do, we often diminish the potential impact that those people can have on us by reaching for a quick hit of dopamine on our phones. But the happiness we feel when we get a new follower or see a photo of an adorable dog fails to provide the biophysical stress release of meaningful interaction with a loved one in real life.

However, the barrier to entry is much lower to open social media, so it's no wonder we jump online again and again to feel connected to others—yet end up feeling lonelier than ever.

THE RISE OF MOBILE DEVICES

The development and expansion of the mobile device market has revolutionized our lives. Although these devices were originally designed strictly for communication, they have changed how we engage with the world at large and even within our own homes and families.

With the expansion of fast and widely available internet access, the growth of handheld and mobile devices exploded. From ever-smaller and lighter laptops to tablets, smartphones, and even smartwatches, it's easier than ever to be constantly connected to the internet.

Round-the-clock access in theory offers unlimited opportunities for connection—yet in reality these devices have become a core source of distraction and ultimately disconnection. The dings and push notifications on our smartphones designed to capture our attention are so effective that even when we don't hear them, we habitually check our phones for notifications.

Mobile devices have also transformed entertainment. Beyond texting with your actual friends, you can watch live streams of other people, read or listen to news or podcasts, and even binge old TV shows or the latest streaming series. The content available at our fingertips often pulls us away from our shared moments and into an individualized virtual experience.

Perhaps the most illustrative example is a family evening:

Meet the Johnsons, a family of four in 1995. The mom is Teri, a twenty-nine-year-old sports and news junkie who loves staying up to date on the day's scores and current events. Her husband, Paul, is twenty-seven. He loves cooking and all things nature. Kate is their five-year-old soccer star who loves cartoons, and three-year-old Elliott wants to be just like his big sister and is currently mastering his colors.

On a cold winter evening after dinner, the family snuggles up together on the sofa to watch TV. Teri grabs the remote and starts toggling through the channel guide. She'd love to catch up on the news but knows the kids would be bored and fighting within minutes. She knows Paul wants to watch a nature show, but she's not in the mood to hear a slow-speaking narrator going on about the migratory patterns of birds she's never heard of. And the thought of watching Kate and Elliott's favorite loud, absurd cartoon would drive her up the wall. As the kids scream out their preferences, Teri and Paul exchange that look when they see what's replaying on one of the cable channels. "Come on, then," Paul says. "Let's watch *The Land Before Time* again."

While Teri may occasionally peek in on the news or Paul's nature show during the movie's commercial breaks, the family is watching the same thing, all together, all at once.

Fast-forward to 2023, and Kate has a son of her own—Ezekiel, who will turn three next month. On a cold winter evening, Kate, her partner, and Ezekiel all gather on the couch for some family time. However, while Kate controls the programming on the main TV, Ezekiel has his own tablet where he's watching child-specific programming on YouTube with his headphones on. Kate's partner scrolls through TikTok on a cell phone. With no one else paying attention to the big TV, Kate simply chooses the show she wants to watch and streams it.

They may all be in the same living room, but they're all facing different directions, having entirely different experiences. They are all consuming content, but none of it is shared. Where once it was common to have a single TV (or two if you were lucky) to entertain an entire family, now every single person can have content specifically tailored to them and their preferences on their personal devices. Culture is siloed. In 1999, a sibling could quote a scene from the most recent episode of a popular network show, and everyone in the family knew the reference instantly. That is no longer the case.

THE EMERGENCE OF "ALWAYS ON" CULTURE

Raise your hand if this sounds familiar. You wake up, roll over, and grab your phone. You turn off the alarm and immediately check notifications, emails, Slack discussions, and calendar reminders. While you get ready for the day, your reminders go off. A meeting is added to your calendar, so you skip lunch or snack at your desk. After you get home, while your partner makes dinner, you try to catch up on tasks. Right before bed, you review the most recent notifications to check one last time before you wake up to do it all again tomorrow.

Globally distributed teams mean we enjoy the benefits of diverse and unique teammates who are best equipped to do the job. It also means that with each new resident of another continent added to your team, they will be working while you're offline, and you might end up getting Slack notifications twenty-four seven. So, if you wait until you log on at 8:00 a.m., you will have a pile of messages to check on. And you have a meeting at 8:15 a.m. There's no way to review everything within your online hours; so what do you do? Well, if you are like most of the professionals we know (including ourselves), you try to stay on top of all those notifications, which leads to checking phones during meals, during family time (while our kids or partners desperately want our attention), and often even as the last thing we do before bed or right when we wake up.

So, while there are reports out there that will tell you with modern technology we are working less than our ancestors, that doesn't account for the reality of the always-online component of modern work. Whether we work remotely or not, our work email and other communication platforms never leave our side—so how can we ever truly unplug from work?

In addition to the notifications-at-your-fingertips feature of modern work that makes it possible to be "always on," employees are feeling increased pressure to work more. A 2023 Harris Poll commissioned by Justworks found that 42 percent of employees are worried about getting laid off, and over 35 percent have started working longer hours due to the economic environment.[18]

Parents, in particular, feel the squeeze: 40 percent of parents with children under eighteen are working longer hours due, in no small part, to the pressures of maintaining a job and health insurance that their young kids depend on.[19] The total annual parental work hours increased by 16 percent (from 2,663 to 3,092 hours) between 1967 and 2009 for the average child in a two-parent family and by 35 percent (938 to 1,262 hours) for the average child in a single-parent family.

The whole picture shows that, unfortunately, we are having a harder and harder time turning work off, and we spend the majority of our waking time working or checking on work.

Work Relationships Matter

Driven by workplace demands, the reduction of traditional connection-building structures (like educational and religious institutions), and the limited social fulfillment offered by digital platforms, more people than ever are turning to work, not only for a paycheck but also for social connection.

For most adults, working is not an option. Work is a fundamental necessity to cover our basic cost of survival. And for many Americans today, that's nearly all that it does. As of September 2023, 62 percent of adults in the US said they are living paycheck to paycheck.[20] With an alarming number of Americans without a single month of living expenses in emergency savings as a result, it's no surprise that a rising number of people around the US are reporting high levels of stress related to their jobs.

Combine this with work taking up so much of our adult lives— not only through time spent on the clock but also the emotional carryover of our workdays seeping into every other aspect of our lives—and we can see the importance of how we design and develop our workplaces is higher than ever. Aside from a life partner, we spend more time with our coworkers than with just about anyone else, according to data. The amount of time we spend at work is staggering. Compared to the time we spend with friends and family, it isn't even close.

Study after study shows a direct link between work relationships and our physical and mental well-being. Beyond providing our salaries, insurance, and other benefits, employers have the opportunity to help their employees live longer, happier, and healthier lives by cultivating strong social bonds and warm connections where we are so heavily invested: at work.

TIME SPENT

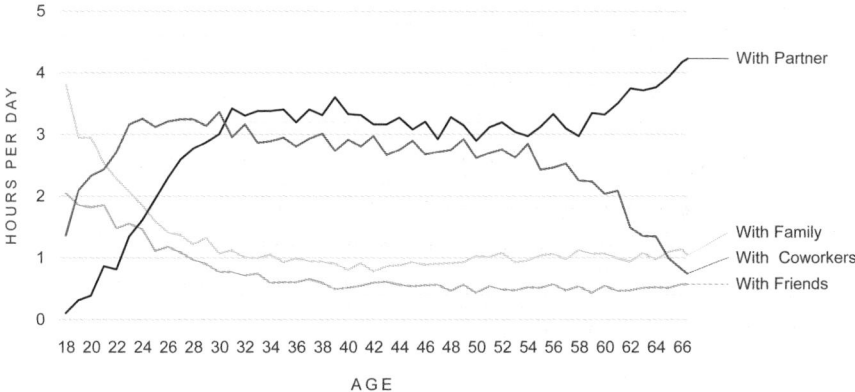

U.S. Bureau of Labor Statistics (2023) – with major processing by Our World in Data. "With family" [dataset].
U.S. Bureau of Labor Statistics, "American Time Use Survey 03-23" [original data].

Anyone who has worked on a team knows that teammates can make or break a work experience. How many of us have fallen out of love with a role but stuck around because of our coworkers? Conversely, how many of us have wanted to leave a job because we could no longer stand our boss even though we enjoyed the work?

Having a good friend and sharing a laugh at work can transform our days, even when faced with a stressful project, yet many of us find it uncomfortable or impossible to get there.

While social interactions in general can be hard, we've made it even harder at work. The pressure to conform to rigid ideas of professionalism and work appropriateness, particularly in certain industries and roles, has discouraged the cultivation of meaningful connections at work. While many corporate compliance handbooks prioritize polite transactional interactions and performative behaviors, the costs are more insidious than we might have imagined.

Masquerading as best practices, some workplace restrictions are designed by bosses trying to control everything from work attire and hairstyles to blacklisted topics and appropriate displays of emotion. When we step back, it's clear how such rules limit our authentic expression, explicitly discouraging vulnerability and limiting opportunities for connection. It's no wonder so many people are playing a part at work instead of being themselves—and feeling more alone than ever.

Restrictive rules limit conversations to low-risk, "work-safe" topics such as food, sports, and hobbies. Inevitably, some teams and individuals will connect more easily around those topics, depending on their comfort level with small talk or passion for pesto. But if we want to have warm connections at work, we need to break through some of these barriers.

Breaking down overtly rigid and antiquated norms does not mean we can do and say anything we want. It is still important to be respectful and honor appropriate boundaries. The best approach is to have rules for engagement on how to show up rather than avoiding connection altogether. This book will provide you with actionable strategies to foster deeper, more meaningful relationships at work and beyond.

CHAPTER 2

Leading by Relationship

Leadership is not about titles, positions, or flowcharts.
It is about one life influencing another.
—John C. Maxwell

These days, people try to pass a lot of things off as leadership. Many people call themselves leaders just because they hold a certain title, position, or status within a company or community—essentially, anyone who's "important" or highly skilled. This is most evident when companies refer to their C-suite as their "leadership team." Then there are self-appointed thought leaders, political party leaders, and even social media influencers who believe that by the transitive property of having social media followers, they qualify as a leader. With more people than ever claiming to be leaders and fewer than ever acting like leaders, we face a global leadership deficit.

Especially in Western cultures, we often recognize individual achievement as if it were carried out in a vacuum, completely independent of others. We prop up "visionaries" such as Steve Jobs and Bill Gates. We forget that while Jobs may have articulated a vision and squeezed performance out of his people, he didn't design the iPhone himself. In fact, if it were up to Jobs alone, the iPhone might've become something very different or failed to exist at all. Bill Gates may have written some of the most important code in the history of computing, but he didn't build Microsoft by himself. Each of these "visionaries" had partners, teams, backers, companies, and entire communities propping them up. Even though they had great ideas, they had to lean into their existing relationships—and create and nurture new ones—to achieve their own versions of success.

Similarly, you may be a genius. You might be charismatic as hell. You may even have a brilliant vision. But if you try to do everything alone, your vision will remain just that: a vision. If you want that vision to become reality, you need the help of other people.

The good news is that others need you as well. We all need more connections and stronger relationships. If you are a task- or accomplishment-oriented leader who prefers to avoid the more personal side of people management, there is no better time to transform your approach. Employee expectations have evolved. People expect more than a paycheck. People expect to work somewhere where they feel respected, fulfilled, and engaged. Transitioning your leadership style away from managing transactions and toward forging connections is the best first step you can take to meet (and exceed) those expectations.

Human-Focused Leadership

Whether we're at work, in our communities, or operating in any other facet of our lives, we need people to step up and be courageous enough to lead, sometimes in uncomfortable and unfamiliar ways. If we want our teams and organizations to thrive in an unknown future, our ideas around what leadership means need to evolve. That's why we're calling for a new type of leadership: human-focused leadership.

Human-focused leadership always comes from a place of service and starts with a question: How will this impact my people? Human-focused leaders accomplish their role-specific tasks—like balancing budgets, hiring and firing, or setting team goals—all while prioritizing the needs and well-being of their people. They see their employees as the business's biggest assets and invest in bringing out the best for and in each employee. It's not an abandonment of operational responsibilities; it's an acknowledgement that their people are what make the organization truly work. It's a shift away from focusing solely on maximizing each employee's outputs and toward maximizing each of their people as a human.

While many traditional managers see themselves as above their teams, human-focused leaders recognize that they are no more important than any other person on the team, regardless of rank or title. They understand that a leader's role is to set the tone and create an environment where everyone is set up to thrive. They recognize that while they have significant influence, they are merely one part of a bigger whole. Whether manager or individual contributor, every person on the team relies on one another to succeed. With our well-being and success on the line, it's crucial for leaders to create human-focused workplaces.

Human-focused workplaces balance fiscal goals and organizational needs with the goals and needs of their individual people, creating conditions where both the organization and its employees can thrive. A core belief of these organizations is that their people are the root of their success.

They are connection-rich environments that empower high-quality inter- and intra-team collaboration and cooperation. They embrace growth mindsets, favor progress over perfection, and strive to be high-learning organizations. They acknowledge the realities of our humanity and go beyond meeting basic needs to set their people up to thrive. They request feedback directly from their people to inform their best practices and honor their individuals. This can look like benefit packages that offer progressive pathways for promotion; inclusive, flexible, and equitable policies; and budget for their people's learning and development. They cultivate a culture where work isn't just a thing you do, but an opportunity to become a more fulfilled, better version of yourself.

These are workplaces where people seek to understand rather than judge. Where team members are encouraged to be their whole selves, not shrink to fit in. Where individuals show up in service of each other rather than only focusing on themselves. Where it's expected to share appreciation, not just criticism. They follow through on their commitments, and they trust their teammates.

These are workplaces that recognize that when they take care of their people, their people take care of the rest. They bring out the best in us individually and collectively. Essentially, they are workplaces that prioritize the human experience, that encourage people to show up fully, treat each other with consideration, and build strong, genuine relationships.

Rethinking Relationships

We think of a relationship as any sort of connection we are trying to establish, maintain, and strengthen over time. We specifically say *over time* because this book is not intended as a guide for quick networking. The very concept of networking is typically tied with transactions—exchanging business cards or contact info to sell something, hire someone, or facilitate other similar business interactions. While it is perfectly normal to start with transactions, this book is about developing genuine relationships that are built to last.

As we consider how to approach our relationships at work, it can be helpful to think of them not as lines between two people, but rather as a triangle. When we think of a relationship simply in terms of you and me, we may be tempted to view it as a zero-sum game. For example, if I allow you to pick where we eat for lunch instead of going where I want to go, next time, it should be my turn to choose—right? I then begin to keep score and might even feel resentment toward you if I feel like I'm "sacrificing" too much. Think about it: How often have you heard that relationships are a give-and-take? Even this terminology implies that you and I will exchange giving and taking from each other.

Seeing a relationship as your way versus my way leads to defensiveness, distance, and tension. While tension may be entertaining in TV and movies, in our everyday relationships, it sets us up—consciously or subconsciously—to compete with one another. Competition inherently increases the probability that we each seek to protect our individual wants and needs above all else and end up viewing the relationship with a zero-sum mindset, which in turn decreases connection. And when relationships become less about connection and more about winning, everyone loses.

The relationship triangle shifts our mindset from sacrificing my wants or needs for yours to intentional compromises that improve our shared well-being. It keeps us grounded as partners, investing in something together, rather than as competitors locked in a zero-sum game.

Three entities exist:

1. You
2. The other person
3. The relationship itself

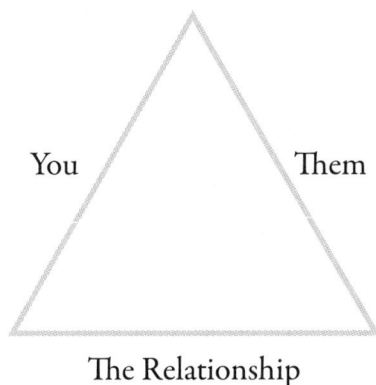

You   Them

The Relationship

When we think about the relationship as its own entity, it's easier to embrace a cooperative position. We are both investing in our collective venture rather than giving up our individual wants for someone else's. As a result, it becomes clear how the time and energy we put into our relationship is directed toward creating something we both benefit from, rather than a loss or sacrifice.

Caring for your relationship is like gardening. Imagine an apple tree, where both partners in a relationship play essential roles in nurturing it: One of you brings the water, and the other provides the sunlight. Although you can both tend to the soil, prune the tree, and add compost, you cannot exchange the sun and water responsibilities. If either party stops showing up, the other might be able to temporarily adjust and make up for the lack of their gardening partner, but sooner rather than later, the tree will begin to struggle, get sick, and ultimately die.

For apple trees, their health and environment dictate their ability to withstand a lack of sunlight and periods of severe drought. One of the reasons we love this metaphor is that relationships develop and take root over time, just like apple trees take time to grow strong and sturdy. Their capacity to withstand violent winds, storms, and even pollution will be dependent on age, root depth, and durability from having weathered smaller storms along the way. Similarly, your relationship's ability to weather conflict, unexpected challenges, and even neglect from one or both parties will depend on the strength and resilience you've developed.

NURTURING THE THREE COMPONENTS OF THE RELATIONSHIP TRIANGLE

Just as apple trees need to be nurtured to grow strong and bear fruit, thriving relationships need to be nurtured as well. Each relationship requires commitments to form the foundation that allows us to grow, weather storms, and ultimately flourish together.

1. **We each must show up for ourselves.**

   Anyone who wants to thrive in a relationship needs to take care of themselves. When we don't take care of ourselves—whether through lack of sleep, poor nutrition, not communicating our needs, or even neglecting our personal development—everything is more challenging. When we are not at our best (physically, emotionally, or otherwise), it is very hard to contribute fully to the other two parts of the triangle.

2. **We each must show up for each other.**

    Showing up when someone wants or needs us is an essential piece of building and nurturing relationships. Beyond our physical presence, what supercharges our ability to relate, connect, and deepen relationships is attunement. As our awareness and responsiveness toward each other's wants and needs increase, we have more opportunities to share moments of joy, laughter, and life's challenges, all of which further bonds us. Without attunement in how we show up, our relationships cannot thrive.

3. **We each must nurture our relationship.**

    The relationship has its own set of needs that cannot be neglected. Relationships need both parties to show up and make time for them; otherwise, a disconnection develops. Imagine this: For the third consecutive week, I'm swamped with work, and you are too. You propose we cancel our one-on-one meeting. Looking at my calendar, I think, *Oh yeah, I really need to catch up on x, y, z; there's nothing absolutely necessary to talk to you about*, and I respond, "Yup! Let's cancel." Each of our individual needs may be met, but our relationship's needs aren't. Over time our connection will suffer and threaten our relationship if we fail to prioritize it.

Ultimately, consideration of each side, intentional action, showing up consistently, and balancing the needs of each side will lead to a healthy, warm, and sustainable relationship.

Leading in a Unique Modern Landscape

While being a human-focused leader is a fulfilling choice, it's not without challenges. Many things can get in our way when we try to inspire and support those around us. Let's zoom out to look at a couple of the circumstantial factors that directly impact leaders today.

A MULTIGENERATIONAL WORKFORCE

One of the common refrains we've heard from clients and industry veterans these past several years is just how hard it is to make their workforce feel unified when they have such a broad range of ages and perspectives working together. While people have been working together across generations since the dawn of modern organizations, the age range has expanded in recent years, introducing some unique challenges.

At the time of writing of this book, the US workforce includes people from all the following generations:

- Baby boomers—born between 1946 and 1964
- Generation X (Gen X)—born between 1965 and 1980
- Millennials (Gen Y)—born between 1981 and 1996
- Generation Z (Gen Z)—born between 1997 and 2012

And we're on the cusp of Generation Alpha (people born after 2012) joining that list. Couple that with an ever-rising average retirement age, and in the next few years, the number of generations working side by side could easily increase to five, which is unprecedented in the modern age.[1]

The difference in social, economic, political, cultural, and—perhaps most importantly—technological climates in which each of these groups was raised cannot be overstated and has a huge impact on their overall values and perspectives. Each group holds varying views on work expectations, quality of life, needs versus wants, relationships, and more. All of this adds up to generations working together who may technically be speaking the same language but still have a difficult time communicating with one another. We each have our own biases about people of other generations, and the corresponding stories we tell ourselves about them can lead us into the trap of us versus them and make collaborating and communicating even harder.

As author Rick Hanson, PhD, points out in his book *Hardwiring Happiness*, "Simply regarding others as 'them,' even when there is no conflict, reduces our capacity for empathy and increases our tendency to dehumanize and devalue those people." And at work, conflict is inevitable. So when teammates of one generation say another "doesn't want to work" or "is antiquated and uptight" or if they spread other broad generalizations, those negative perceptions drive division.

And when we are divided, it's easy to focus on what divides us rather than what unites us. This is why it's so important for us as leaders to remember that despite individual differences, team members have more in common with one another than not. While, for example, we each may define success and fulfillment differently, we all want to feel successful and fulfilled. So as a leader of a multigenerational team whose members are held back by prejudices or misconceptions and are struggling to work with one another, you have to facilitate effective and meaningful communication to cultivate a culture of collaboration and strengthen interpersonal relationships.

Though improved communication skills can help us better navigate many generational disconnects, the most impactful assets for misaligned teams are strong relationships between all team members, not only between the leader and those they lead. When we forge strong connections with one another, we are better able to give and receive feedback. We are less scared to ask questions that might make us feel silly or stupid (*What is a "rizz"?*). And we see more value in overcoming the obstacles and perceived barriers between us. We may never get everyone on the team speaking the same language, but we can at least help create an environment where the team prioritizes understanding one another.

Human-focused leadership helps bridge gaps, increase communication, discourage judgment, and create alignment—all of which you will see in the subsequent chapters. Another impactful strategy that human-focused leaders can leverage is defining team norms and expectations. People who have organizational authority (a.k.a. "bosses") can set standards and expectations that span generations. Clear guidelines for communications, mutual support, and accountability go a long way to bridging some of these intergenerational gaps.

ON-SITE, REMOTE, OR HYBRID TEAMS

Communities—and more specifically, offices—were once largely bound by geography. Friends, family, and coworkers lived in the same city or general area. Your closest friends were often literally your closest friends. Now we have virtual communities more focused on common interests than proximity.

Even just twenty-five years ago, the typical office was a single campus where all employees had to physically come to work. In such an environment, it felt easier to get a read on someone through tone of voice, body language, and witnessing their interactions with different people in different scenarios. Plus, if you wanted to get to know someone better, you could grab lunch or coffee together when you were on break.

Workplace Models: What's the Difference?

On-Site | All work is expected to be done on location. All employees work in physical offices or meet on-site at client or partner offices 100 percent of the time.

Fully Remote | This generally means one of three things: working from a home office, working at an agreed-upon coworking office or location (such as a specific geographic region), or working from anywhere, as long as the internet connection is strong and stable enough.

Hybrid | This is perhaps the most nebulous term because there are so many variations. It can mean working a certain number of days per week (or month or year) in an office and working all other days from home. It can also mean the company allows employees to work an allotted amount of time from anywhere in the world but requires attendance at a corporate location when they happen to be in town.

Today it's easier than ever to have exclusively virtual relationships with colleagues or clients. In fact, many of us today have friends and colleagues from around the world that we've never even met in person, only through email, texts, video chat, or other social tools.

This is often a tough adjustment for leaders, especially those who developed their leadership style through managing a team of people who all worked together on a single floor of a physical office building. Technological advances that enabled remote work disrupted entire industries and changed what work looks like. As with any massive disruption, diverging opinions on what to do next have led to opposing pressures and influences on leaders of remote-capable teams. For instance, many local governments and shareholders are pushing companies to mandate in-person office work. Simultaneously, current and potential employees are largely demanding hybrid or fully remote work guarantees. To stay competitive as an employer in today's job market, it can feel like you're in the middle of a tug-of-war where no matter what you do, you lose.

With increased global competition and organizations operating across multiple borders (cultural, geographic, linguistic, and political), managing remote work can feel daunting. Even if you want to offer full remote flexibility for your team—and there are no legal or security reasons not to—how do you reasonably manage a distributed workforce?

Discuss expectations for attendance and availability, amount of hours online vs. set working times, norms around handling interruptions, response times, etc., tool and platform usage (which types of communications are sent via which methods—email, Microsoft Teams chat, text messages, phone calls, or in-person), acceptable levels of formality (in writing to clients, in conversation with one another, in dress, during client calls, etc.), and ways to address and resolve interpersonal tensions. Creating alignment requires clear communication with everyone and importantly, not aligning all rules and expectations to just one generation or individual's preferences (including and especially yours). Additionally, explaining the reasoning behind these boundaries is crucial. And don't forget to involve your people in crafting these expectations! They can help you find the ideal mix for your team.

SAFETY

Interpersonal physical safety and psychological safety are baseline requirements for healthy relationships.

Physical Safety

Physical violence, especially toward women, is alarmingly pervasive in the US and globally. In the United States, one in three women and one in four men have experienced some form of physical violence from an intimate partner. Every minute, an average of twenty-four people are abused by an intimate partner. According to the director-general of the World Health Organization, "Violence against women is endemic in every country and culture, causing harm to millions of women and their families."[2] And due to the shame and stigma that prevent reporting and getting care after an assault, experts estimate the true numbers are far higher.

What does this mean for our working relationships? Statistically speaking, if you are not personally affected by violence, it's likely multiple people you work with are—and awareness of this probability must inform company culture. When you decide on company policies or plan company retreats or social events, assume you have abuse survivors among the members of your staff. Make it clear you're dedicated to healthy boundaries and respecting one another's physical space so that everyone feels as physically safe as possible at work and work events.[3]

Psychological Safety

Harvard Business School professor Amy Edmondson defines psychological safety as "a shared belief held by members of a team that it's okay to take risks, to express their ideas and concerns, to speak up with questions, and to admit mistakes—all without fear of negative consequences." Edmondson also coined the term "team psychological safety," and describes it as "felt permission for candor."[4]

Psychological safety creates the foundation for team members to openly communicate, improve collaboration, and embrace the courage needed to create and innovate. And to reach team psychological safety throughout our organizations, it must be cocreated, visibly supported by everyone including senior executives, and intentionally fostered over time. Psychological safety is essential for high employee engagement, which, in addition to the human benefits, also benefits the bottom line. In their 2025 report, Gallup estimates if the workforce was fully engaged, it could unlock $9.6 trillion USD in productivity, which represents 9 percent of global GDP.[5]

Power Dynamics

Safety and power are inextricably linked. How empowered or disempowered we feel directly affects how we show up, interact with one another, and assess safety in situations and spaces.

When one person ranks higher than another on the organizational chart, the power dynamic is overt, and how it directly influences the relationship is clearer. Even in cases where we might not notice a hierarchy, we may just lack the vantage point to see it. Beyond formal hierarchies—such as manager versus direct reports and senior versus junior roles—informal hierarchies also have significant influence. Informal hierarchies can include things like socio-economic class, friendships with higher-ups, or even age and educational background.

When a team has a large power discrepancy between teammates, it is essential to acknowledge and address it. If those with power don't notice or appreciate that others are disempowered, or act accordingly to address it, there is a very low chance for team psychological safety. Once there is awareness of the power dynamics affecting the team, those with power can leverage their influence to remove obstacles that diminish others' power. Together we can work to create a more equitable culture by making it safe to show up and be candid without fear of repercussions. If you want to catalyze such a change, don't forget: the bigger burden of action rests on the person with more power.

Essentially, if you could fire Hakim, or easily leverage your influence to get Hakim fired, you are the one who must make the effort to create a safe space for Hakim to be candid. This is an uncomfortable truth for many leaders to face: Your actions have the potential to disempower your people. The upside is that you have the power to create safety and empower all of your people instead.

While our modern work context presents unique challenges and is evolving rapidly, we can find solutions if we are willing to show up as human-focused leaders. And perhaps the best news we can offer is that you can implement everything we outline in this book, whether you're sitting together in the same room or thousands of miles apart. You can help people connect and align across any and all age groups. And you can make sure that both physical and psychological safety are priorities on your team. But it doesn't happen by chance—we have to be intentional about the spaces we create for our people.

A Leader's Potential for Impact

As leaders—especially those who manage people—our ability to impact others is massive. Gallup research has found that 70 percent of the variance in team engagement is tied to management.[6] Management behaviors are by far the single most influential and impactful component of employee engagement: Our relationships with our bosses can make or break our working experience.

But there's more to it than that. It turns out that relationships between managers and employees can have a huge impact on an employee's overall health. A survey of over three thousand employees in Sweden found that those who worked for bad bosses were 60 percent more likely to suffer a stroke, heart attack, or other life-threatening cardiac condition; while other studies show that people with bad bosses are more susceptible to chronic depression, stress, and anxiety.[7] Thus, it's not an overstatement to say that if we aren't taking care of our employees, we're not just doing a disservice to our workforce—we are diminishing their quality of life and reducing lifespans.

With so much at stake, it's more important now than ever to invest in addressing these challenges individually and as a team. As a leader, you have the power to catalyze the change needed on a bigger scale than most. That power to transform begins with transforming yourself and your leadership to be more human focused. This approach must be lived from the inside out.

It requires unlearning behaviors that no longer serve you, going beyond checking off items on a to-do list, and relearning how to set your team up for success. The journey to becoming a human-focused leader takes time, effort, intention, and a whole lot of self-grace. Shifting toward human-focused leadership will best equip you to tackle the most daunting leadership challenges of today and tomorrow. And to help you get there, the coming chapters outline five principles designed to hone your leadership abilities and create stronger relationships with those around you. We call them the **five embodiments.**

CHAPTER 3

What Is an Embodiment?

If we are aware that our manners—language, behavior, and actions—are measured against our values and principles, we are able to more easily embody the philosophy that leadership is a matter of how to be, not how to do.

—Frances Hesselbein

We've chosen the term *embodiment* very much by design. Often, even our most cherished ideas remain merely conceptual when we think of them only as principles or values, but embodiment brings those concepts to life. Embodiment is a principle personified. It is tangible. It is felt and active, blending the internal and external aspects of our principles and values. Embodiment requires cognizance, physical awareness, attention, and action. To live these embodiments means representing them in action, not just in thought or word. This is especially critical for leaders since our actions, behaviors, and words carry significant influence. Even our whisper is a shout.

The Path to Embodiment

AWARENESS ➤ PRACTICE ➤ HABIT ➤ EMBODIMENT

The first step on the path to embodiment is *awareness*. We need to know which principles and values we wish to embody before we can bring them to life. Once we become aware of them, we must intentionally begin to put these principles into *practice*. Practice is intentionally acting on our principles throughout each day. With patience and repetition, a practice turns into a healthy *habit*, something we do that doesn't require active thought or need to be interjected into our days. As we expand our habits, they further influence how we see and interact with the world on a deeper level. Ultimately when the principle becomes an essential part of who we are and how we show up—regardless of circumstance—we reach *embodiment*.

Simple enough, right? We're not proposing anything complicated, yet we know this work is far from easy. At a glance, you may feel like you already live some of these embodiments, which is great. But even if you're crushing it in some areas, there is always room to improve. As a team, one of our core tenets is "no final drafts" (#NFD), which reminds us to keep iterating. The concept of NFD is rooted in our dedication to a growth mindset. Even something we deeply cherish and think we have done well may need to be edited and improved later. So keep writing in pencil, and keep learning.

Sometimes the simplest truths we wholeheartedly believe are the hardest to embody. We can tell you to practice curiosity or show people that you care, and so on. But to change habits that no longer serve us, adjust behaviors, and truly embody these values takes long-term commitment. Embodiment requires presence and intention; in any given moment you can check in with yourself to assess if you're in alignment with the principles you aim to embody.

Why We Chose These Embodiments

So why five embodiments—and why *these* five? As we did our research for this book, we examined not only our lived experience but also client interviews, industry surveys, and data from various fields and found what strengthens interpersonal connection falls into one or more of the following:

- Curiosity
- Authenticity
- Care
- Gratitude
- Ownership

These simple principles have anything but simple aspirations. Each embodiment plays a crucial role in building, maintaining, and enhancing our relationships and addressing the loneliness and low-engagement crises. While each embodiment has independent value, it's the interconnection of these five that weaves a strong yet flexible foundation to develop the warm relationships we need to live a long and healthy life. At work, this looks like employees with high levels of engagement, well-being, and connection.

We've ordered the following chapters intentionally. Each section will help to lay a foundation for the one that follows. Each embodiment is inevitably intertwined with the others, so you may find that an embodiment from one chapter is enhanced by an embodiment from a later chapter or two. However, we've done our best to lay out the chapters in a way that'll help you gather some serious building blocks for each subsequent embodiment—especially if these are largely new or underused concepts in your daily life, or when a relationship is new.

All five of these embodiments play a crucial role in forging stronger bonds with one another. Curiosity opens the door to understanding; authenticity is core to belonging; care grounds us in service; gratitude shifts our focus to appreciation; and ownership fosters trust. Your dedicated energy and attention to each and how they interact will be vital to the success you have in building connections with others.

What to Know Before Diving In

As we dive into some of the nuances around each embodiment, we hope you'll pick up a few tips and tricks to bring them to life in an even more powerful way. But before we move forward, we'd like to cover a few important things to keep in mind.

LEAD BY EXAMPLE

Relationships take work on all sides, and while the healthiest relationships come from all participants working on each embodiment, we encourage you to focus on how *you* live each embodiment. Focus on what you can control, and you will maximize your impact! By showing up and practicing these embodiments, you are inherently inviting everyone around you to join the path to embodiment. In our experience, the best way to extend an invitation is to model the behavior.

BUILD ON YOUR VALUES

The embodiments will not work as replacements for your personal values or ethical code. The embodiments are a method of moving through life in a way that adds to your existing values and ethics. For example, if a personal core value of yours is ambition, that's completely compatible with the five embodiments. You can be ambitious and implement what we cover in this book. Also, keep in mind that these embodiments are not an exhaustive list of everything you can do to enhance your relationships—that would be a book without an ending. Think of these, rather, as universal principles you can apply to your life whenever and wherever you are.

START WITH A SHARED UNDERSTANDING

As you get into the embodiment chapters, you'll notice we begin by providing our definition for each embodiment. We know that each of us sees the world differently, and yet it's sometimes hard to remember that. When we're lost in the confusion of a difficult interaction, it's easy to get overwhelmed. *How can they not see what I'm seeing?* we wonder, forgetting that each of us sees through our own unique lens.

JEAN

When I was around eight years old, I remember being utterly confused when my teenage brother came home from the optometrist's office. The tree in front of our deck had been there our entire lives, but that day, looking through new glasses, my brother gazed at its branches in awe. "It has leaves!" he shouted. To me, the tree looked like it had always looked. *Of course it has leaves*, I thought. But what appeared to be an ordinary tree to me was an exciting revelation for my brother. Until then, he had spent years in a blurry world.

Our lived experiences and unique lenses are foundational to our perceptions of the world and everything in it (especially our relationships). It's the color and texture of the relational painting. Not being able to fully enunciate our experience with shared language is like trying to describe a Picasso without referring to symbolism, brush styles, or technique. If we can remember that people perceive colors and textures in starkly different ways, perhaps we can stay compassionate rather than accusatory when someone doesn't see something the way we do. We then might begin to bridge the gap between our different versions of the world and be on our way to a common understanding.

We start each embodiment chapter by sharing our definition of each term because of our desire to work from a shared understanding that's grounded in the real-world context of human relationships. While they may not match the dictionary, we're not suggesting that *Oxford* or *Merriam-Webster* have it wrong. It's more a reflection of our belief that language is alive and evolving.

GIVE YOURSELF GRACE

We are all imperfect works in progress. It's important to remember this as you pursue growth in any important area, which can be difficult, especially if you have perfectionist tendencies. A helpful way to navigate these moments with grace is separating the deed and the doer. One of Matt's favorite roles is uncle, and this is a lesson he's recently shared with his nephews:

A few years back, my nephews (aged eight and eleven at the time) wanted to work on their basketball skills, so I took them to run a few drills at the nearby gym.

In one drill, I had the boys start about twenty feet away from the basket. They would dribble the ball a few times with their dominant hand, perform a crossover into their weak hand, come to a jump stop, and then shoot the ball at the hoop. After running the drill a few times, both boys were having trouble crossing the ball over from their dominant hand to their weak hand. Each time they lost control of the ball or missed a shot, they would mutter phrases like, "I can't do this!" or "I'm the worst."

After a few of these comments, I stopped the drill: "Hold up. Why do you both keep saying such mean things about yourselves?"

The boys looked at each other. "Because we keep messing it up! It's too hard," one vented.

"Yeah, we suck," his brother chimed in.

Sensing their frustration and seeing an opportunity for a learning moment, I crouched to their eye level and said, "Hold on. That dribble may have sucked, but *you* don't suck. You just need to work on it."

"We know . . ." they moaned, still clearly frustrated.

"Just because that may have felt like one of your worst shots doesn't make *you* the worst."

I could see that it was starting to click for them as they looked back at me and nodded, silently.

"I'll tell you something that my basketball coach told me back in high school when I was getting frustrated and wanted to give up. He said, 'We all screw up. That's how we learn and get better. But messing up isn't the same as being a screwup. You aren't your mistakes.' Do you guys understand?"

Their smiles came back as they both gave out a relieved "Yeah," and we started the drill back up.

The same is true for each of us in our daily practice of the embodiments. As you read about what gets in the way of embodying these principles, you may find yourself thinking, *Wait. I do that. Am I the problem?* If one of these thoughts occurs to you, it's important to recognize that, sure, you may have some bad habits you need to refine or eliminate. Who doesn't? Who you are is not only determined by your worst habits. The deed (even the occasional repetitive or habitual deed) is not the same thing as who you are as the doer. You can change. You can choose. If a behavior or mindset is getting in the way of bringing an embodiment to life, and you recognize it, you have already taken an important first step toward correcting it. As long as you're open to acknowledging areas for improvement and adjusting accordingly, you're already well on your way to becoming the best version of yourself and building healthier relationships.

Throughout the process, it is important to remind ourselves that we all deserve some grace. No one is immune to having a bad day or making a mistake. Reaching embodiment is about shifting our default settings, not striving for perfection. We will inevitably fall short of our best selves sometimes. The question isn't if we fall short; it's how we handle the situation when we do. In a moment when we are tired and hungry or just fought with our spouse, we are all capable of saying a careless thing to a colleague. If we address it, acknowledge the reason we were in a bad mood (not a lack of care for them but our hunger or marital issues), and make amends, it reinforces our integrity and shows this person that they can trust us to embody care even, and especially, after a mistake.

We're in this together. We're here for growth and improvement, not judgment. We all have plenty of unhealthy habits we'd like to change, and while sometimes our behaviors are awkward or out of alignment with our values, it's important not to fall into the trap of conflating what we do and who we are.

As we've pointed out already, this work is not easy. However, it does get easier. As you begin to build the muscles associated with each embodiment, even when you fall short or miss the mark, you'll still be moving deeper into connection with others. So take a deep breath, accept your imperfections, and prepare to tackle the challenge of becoming a human-focused leader, strengthening your relationships, and creating a workplace that doesn't suck.

CHAPTER 4

Embodiment #1: Curiosity

The mind that opens to a new idea never returns to its original size.
—**Albert Einstein**

**Curiosity is an appetite to explore and learn
more in order to better understand the world,
the people around us, and ourselves.**

When you hear the word *curiosity*, what images come to mind? Is it a young child constantly asking their parent, "But why?" Maybe you envision a cat looking puzzled at a new toy. Perhaps it's a student in a classroom with a raised hand. While curiosity is often seen as simply asking questions or wondering, that's just the beginning. It's also a mindset—a truly transformative one— that recognizes no matter how much we know, there is always more to learn.

When we are curious, we begin with questions rather than assumptions, which allows us to uncover information that we otherwise couldn't see. It reduces our tendency to fall back onto biases and allows us to see things with open eyes. As such, curiosity can break down walls between people, build bridges of understanding, and open doors to the unknown. Before any successful invention, rather than looking at a problem and just assuming it was a permanent obstacle, the inventor asks, "How might I solve this problem?" And when a teacher or peer told them something wasn't possible, rather than simply saying okay and moving on, they asked, "Why not?" Curiosity keeps us thinking about the possibilities and solutions rather than getting fixated on obstacles.

Think about how this applies to the three sides of our relationship triangle.

Cultivating curiosity within *yourself* is the antidote for "this is just the way I am." Each time we have a strong reaction or leap to judgment, it's an opportunity to get curious about ourselves, our perspectives, and what drives those behaviors. Through self-reflection we improve our self-awareness and self-compassion, which is key to our own development as well as a prerequisite to giving anyone else our unofficial operating manual (think: instructions for how to best connect with me). As leaders, it's especially important that we increase our awareness of how our lived experiences influence our expectations and interactions with our people.

Curiosity about other people and their perspectives transforms how we understand, relate, and collaborate with them. When we don't let assumptions dictate our next move, we stop judgment, disconnection, and the blame game in their tracks. When we show up curious to get to know others, we learn more about them, gain a deeper understanding of who they are, and hear interesting context and insights we'd often otherwise miss. Beyond what we can learn that helps us better connect and strengthen our relationship, curiosity creates a pull in the relationship because it demonstrates interest and makes others feel seen and heard.

Curiosity about the relationship side helps us discover previously unearthed needs and expectations. When we inquire about the relationship entity, we expand the dialogue, allowing us to sit side by side and better understand it together, rather than from opposite sides. For example, even asking a simple question such as, "What does 'mentor' mean to you?" can uncover differences in expectations that are often under the surface. With curious intentionality, we can cocreate and nurture a relationship we both individually benefit from.

Through this process, we are better able to identify and address potential issues before and as they arise. It grounds us in commitment to one another, reminding us that we are partners investing in something together rather than being on opposite sides in a zero-sum game. It allows us to explore the dynamic we are creating together instead of simply focusing on each individual separately.

For example, let's say I've been getting what I personally need, and you have too, but something still feels off. Using curiosity helps us explore the disconnect. Through being curious about myself and about you, we realize we both avoid conflict. By also checking in on what our relationship needs, we realize we have been avoiding hard conversations that would benefit the relationship. We can now make a plan together. Through curious investigation, we are now able to meet a previously unknown relationship need and prevent further disconnection.

Curiosity opens the door to forming connections and deepening our understanding of our individual and relational needs. When you engage with someone through the lens of curiosity, it automatically creates a pull in the relationship dynamic. The more curious we get about ourselves, the other person, and our relationship, the more potential there is for conversation. The more breadth and depth of conversation, the more opportunities for connection. And the more diverse our connections with one another are, the stronger the relationship becomes.

Leadership author John C. Maxwell once said, "Leadership is not about titles, positions, or flowcharts. It is about one life influencing another."[1] Our ability to influence those we wish to lead is directly tied to the strength of our connection. And embodying curiosity invites connection with the people around you. It supercharges your ability to have maximum impact and influence.

Curiosity challenges us to think beyond our assumptions and ask better questions. When we ask a question based in assumption ("You look bothered; what's up?"), we invite defensiveness and disconnection. However, when we shift to open questions ("What's on your mind?"), we invite conversation and connection.

Asking multiple-choice or yes-or-no questions limits the number of ways someone can respond. When we ask open-ended questions, it allows them to respond however they see fit, and we can often learn more than we might expect.

For example, let's say the boss just yelled at a colleague in a meeting. You want to check in on your colleague afterward, so you decide to ask them about it. Let's look at a few possible questions and see which one best embodies a sense of curiosity about how your colleague feels:

1. Did the boss yelling at you make you mad? (yes or no)
2. Were you more embarrassed or angry? (multiple choice)
3. How did that experience make you feel? (open-ended)

The first two options only give them a couple of ways to answer. In question one, you'll only know whether your colleague was mad or not. Question two only invites them to tell you if they were embarrassed or angry. But what if they wouldn't describe their emotions in either of those ways? What if what they really felt was a sense of betrayal? What if they felt that the boss had let them down? Neither of the first two questions gives them the option to share their thoughts in their own words. Only question number three does that. Open-ended questions fully engage the people we are talking to and help us remember that they may have an entirely different answer to offer than the options we think up on our own. This is why open-ended questions are such valuable tools in our curiosity toolbelt.

Curious Leadership

Curious leaders shift the entire team dynamic.

Picture this. You're a volunteer for the parents' association at your child's school. This school year, they've asked that all volunteers serve on at least one event committee. Right now, two different committees exist, headed by two very different committee chairs—let's call them Dan and Arya. Dan has a reputation for being a know-it-all. He doesn't ask for advice or help or admit when he doesn't know something. When Dan kicks off the committee's initial meeting, he dictates his vision of what he wants the event to look like, and he never asks for input from the team. He doesn't seem interested in finding out what other people think, or even what roles they might want to play on the committee. Dan just gives out orders and assignments.

Meanwhile, on Arya's committee, she begins by asking what role you'd like to play. She asks if you have ideas for the year's event and how she can best support you and set you up for success. She speaks to questions she feels confident answering but freely admits when she doesn't have the answer. In fact, she joins the asker in a quest to find an answer. Arya's willingness to admit she doesn't know everything signals that she is more interested in growth and improvement than in being right. Her transparency and clear intention to unite the group exemplify open, flexible, and curious leadership.

Something else that Arya signals through her actions is humility. When you ask people about the most important characteristics of a leader, humility consistently makes the list. A 2016 study found that humility was positively correlated with leadership effectiveness, as rated by both leaders and their subordinates.[2] And a 2018 review of decades of research on humility and leadership concluded that humble leaders are more likely to be seen as effective and inspiring by their followers.[3] At its core, humility, like curiosity, requires recognition that you don't know everything and that there are always new ways to grow and improve. No matter what stage of life or career you're in, curiosity and humility send the message you're interested in finding the best path forward rather than being the one with the answers.

Compare this to the messages Dan's actions are sending. He is unwilling to listen, ask for help, or admit he's unsure. He has no interest in seeking input from others. Dan's actions make it clear that his priority is doing the event on his terms and that he's uninterested in his committee members' thoughts or ideas. He's demonstrating the very opposite of human-focused leadership.

Demanding people do as they're told, as Dan did kills curiosity and often leads to making rash, ill-advised decisions. For example, while the decorations volunteer had the foresight to ask the A/V volunteer to share budget to get a tent in case of rain, they decided that neither of them was willing to challenge Dan (who was adamant it wouldn't rain). After rain ruined the rentals, Dan refused to acknowledge his part, blamed the volunteers, and left the school with debt and a damaged reputation.

Curiosity isn't just a leadership skill; it's the foundation of connection, innovation, and growth. When we embrace curiosity, we don't just become better leaders; we build stronger, more human-focused workplaces and relationships.

Cultivating a Culture of Curiosity

The more curious we are, the more expansive our world becomes—both as individuals and as teams. As we've outlined in this chapter, whether between managers and direct reports or among teammates, interpersonal curiosity can radically transform our communication, preventing misunderstandings and wasting time working against ourselves. But when we leverage it at the team-wide level, we accelerate adoption and catalyze the very types of connections that transform our work and our lives.

Most organizations already prize the results of applying

curiosity to things like product development, market analysis, and general problem-solving. In addition to the day-in and day-out benefits, curiosity also increases resilience and adaptability when facing challenges. Curiosity helps us put on our scientist coats to evaluate, assess, hypothesize, and resolve problems. When we understand the problem and ask, "What can we do to right the ship?" we naturally shift our focus toward collaboration rather than accusations, blame, or unproductive complaints—which propels us forward together.

When curiosity goes beyond task- or problem-based applications and becomes an integral part of how each team member shows up, we don't just better innovate and problem solve; we become a stronger team. We transform our relationship with mistakes and embrace the wisdom of intelligent failures. When an entire team feels the shift toward curiosity and experiences its benefits firsthand, we dismantle defensiveness, stonewalling, shaming, blaming, and all of the other ways we try to protect ourselves when we fear being wrong. The resulting ripple effects of a culture of curiosity extend to improved team communication, trust, cooperation, and alignment.

Workplaces that value curiosity build environments, and even systems, that empower team members to wonder, ask questions, and test theories before jumping to solutions. These can include things like team norms about asking questions before making statements after proposals, time built into meetings for contemplation about how ideas *could* work, and even dedicated meetings to explore what we as a team could be missing. When we weave curiosity into the fabric of our organizations, we chart our path toward becoming a high-learning, continually improving, innovative leader in our field.

What Gets in the Way

While curiosity has many benefits, the learning curve to becoming more curious is often steeper than we'd like it to be. Fully embracing curiosity can take time—not for lack of desire or effort but because a lot of ingrained and even culturally celebrated behaviors get in the way. Let's explore some of the most common obstacles.

UNCHARITABLE ASSUMPTIONS

When we make uncharitable assumptions, we often set into motion a cycle of judgment, defensiveness, and criticism, which ultimately, drives disconnection. Let's say you decide to get a decadent dessert after dinner even after your partner warned you that it would give you a stomachache. Sure enough, about an hour later, you're holding your stomach in discomfort. Your partner notices, makes eye contact, and opens their mouth to speak. You assume they are about to say they told you so, and before they can utter a single word, you beat them to the punch. "I already know what you're going to say," you bark. "Don't."

Or maybe there's an upcoming family event that requires formal attire. You just know that your sweatpants-wearing teen will have an issue with it. "Before you even ask, no, you can't just wear athletic attire," you say. "We need to be dressed nice as a family for once."

In either scenario, how do you imagine your assumptions felt to the other party? The fact that you cut them off based on what you assumed they'd say robbed them of the option to pleasantly surprise you.

Assumptions are the ego's attempt at fortune-telling. They are the brain's way of using a shortcut so it can conserve energy for other survival functions. In a 2017 TED Talk, psychology professor Lisa

Feldman Barrett explained it this way: "Predictions are primal. . . . They help us to make sense of the world in a quick and efficient way. So your brain does not react to the world. Using past experience, your brain predicts and constructs your experience of the world."[4]

So making assumptions is a natural and often helpful thing for our brains to do. However, when we act as if our uncharitable assumptions are facts—whether we're right or not—it can damage the relationship, especially when it becomes habitual. We never know the internal experience of another person. We can't know what they think or feel, and when we think we can, we turn off the part of our brain that sees value in learning beyond our personal sphere of knowledge. We kill curiosity. We eliminate wonder. We rob ourselves and other people of the possibilities the world has to offer.

SEEKING CERTAINTY

The human brain, specifically our neocortex, is hardwired to make sense of the world around us so that it can keep us safe and alive. Because of this, we are compelled to seek certainty in a complex world. Unfortunately, the real world is unpredictable. As such, certainty is unrealistic. Seeking and clinging to certainty creates another obstacle to practicing curiosity.

To our brain, danger is danger—physical or not. This is why we struggle when things out of our control affect us negatively, like the global economy or the opinions of others. Our brain needs to feel like it can solve the problem of unpredictability, but it can't. Does that stop us from trying though? Absolutely not. Biological and cultural influences conflate certainty with safety in an attempt to simplify a complex world. This is why there is such a seductive transition from assumptions to certainty. And once we get to a place

Practice Makes Progress

INDIVIDUAL PRACTICES

Try the 80/20 Rule

In conversations, aim to spend at least 80 percent of your time listening and asking questions, while only making statements or giving answers up to 20 percent of the time. This naturally puts your brain into learning mode because it's trying to understand something or someone. While this isn't something you can do with everyone all the time (sometimes, for example, you just need to make a decision or give information), you'll be surprised at how often you can utilize it in your daily interactions!

Ask Better Questions

It's not enough to simply ask more questions when aiming to improve your curiosity. The depth of our curiosity is often reflected more in the quality of our questions than the quantity. Great questions have the potential to do more than just give us confirmation of what we already do or do not think. They create the opportunity for others to give us context and help us see a clearer picture of the world around us. We can improve our questions in a couple of ways:

- **Default to open-ended questions.** During our workdays, even if it's unintentional, many of us default to closed-ended questions with yes/no or multiple-choice answers. While these questions can be very efficient and useful when looking for validation of facts, as we mentioned above, they limit the ways that the other person can respond.

- **Ask more clarifying questions (encourage expansion/ digging deeper).** When someone shares a new or differing perspective, you have an opportunity to engage your curiosity. Rather than assuming your language and intent are aligned with the other person, try asking:

  » Can you share more about _____?
  » What do you mean by _____?
  » What is your interpretation of _____?
  » Say more . . .
  » What I am hearing is . . . [share what you believe they are saying]. What am I missing?

Pivot Toward Generous Assumptions

Unlike uncharitable assumptions that hinder curiosity, generous assumptions can encourage it. Our brain's primary function is to keep us alive, so it's natural that it looks for potential danger and tries to get us to notice concerning behaviors. But we have the power to combat that initial impulse. Generous assumptions are invitations to ourselves to challenge impulsive reactions and negative judgments. Let's look at some examples:

- A guy in a pickup truck cuts you off in traffic without using a blinker.

  » Uncharitable assumption: He's a jerk and doesn't care about anyone else on the road.
  » Generous assumption: Maybe he didn't see me, or he could be in a rush because there's an emergency.

- Your normally chatty best work-friend is quiet and unresponsive today when you try to engage in conversation with him.

  » Uncharitable assumption: Wow, he's being so rude. I bet he doesn't like me anymore.
  » Generous assumption: Maybe he's having a hard day or has a headache and needs quiet.

Notice that in both examples, the generous assumptions are rooted in the idea that we cannot know the full picture, whereas the uncharitable assumptions leap to judgment.

TEAM-WIDE PRACTICES

Implement a Curiosity Reminder

Since judgment and the illusion of certainty can be so damaging to curiosity, it's important that we help our team members address these issues as they happen. It can be hard to call people out in the moment, especially for those of us who struggle with directness and confrontation, so it's helpful to implement a team-wide signal word or phrase that indicates a request for more curiosity (as opposed to the judgment or lack of openness they might be feeling) in any given moment. This can be something obvious and direct, such as saying, "Calling for curiosity," or something random and silly, like saying, "Biscuits!" You could even designate a silent gesture, like a double hand raise, to signal that curiosity is needed. Invite the team to come together to develop the signal, and then hold it sacred.

Celebrate the Assist

Most of our teams and organizations are great at celebrating when people find the right answer, but we aren't very good at celebrating when someone asks the right question to assist in finding that answer. When someone in a meeting asks an insightful or crucial question, call it out! When we reward behavior, we often get more of that behavior, so give some positive reinforcement to people who embody curiosity throughout the day. You can even turn this into an award if you'd like, which can be celebrated and recognized weekly, monthly, or quarterly.

Challenge Assumptions

We must get in the habit of challenging our assumptions in multiple facets of life—not just in our one-on-one relationships. One place you can try this out is during meetings. When discussing decisions in meetings, always make sure to ask, "For this to be true, what assumptions are we making here?" Have the group go through the elements of the decision-making process such as budget, market sentiment, team availability, and datasets. As assumptions begin to surface, make sure to ask, "How can we challenge these?" The act of inviting these challenges reminds us to keep a curious mind.

CURIOSITY SNAPSHOT 📷

OUR DEFINITION

Curiosity is an appetite to explore and learn more in order to better understand the world, the people around us, and ourselves.

KEY TAKEAWAYS

- No matter how much we know, there is always more to learn.
- Showing up and practicing curiosity breaks down walls and disconnections based on judgment, uncharitable assumptions, biases, and more.
- Turning curiosity inward helps us increase our self-awareness, leading to better opportunities for growth, self-compassion, and language to share our operating manual with others.
- Curious leaders create inclusive, collaborative environments where humility, openness, and shared understanding flourish.
- Embedding curiosity into team culture improves resilience, communication, and innovation while dismantling defensiveness and blame.
- Curiosity is foundational for an open-minded approach to connecting with others, inviting diverse perspectives, and trying new experiences.

WHAT GETS IN THE WAY

- Uncharitable assumptions
- Seeking certainty
- Judgment
- A need to prove
- Familiarity and experience

PRACTICE MAKES PROGRESS

- **Individual practices**
  - Try the 80/20 rule.
  - Ask better questions.
    - Start with open-ended questions.
    - Ask more clarifying questions.
  - Pivot toward generous assumptions.

- **Team-Wide Practices**
  - Implement a curiosity reminder.
  - Celebrate the assist.
  - Challenge assumptions.

CHAPTER 5

Embodiment #2: Authenticity

The privilege of a lifetime is being who you are.
—Joseph Campbell

**Authenticity is showing up as your truest self—
the intersection of self-awareness, honesty, and vulnerability.**

As human beings, we need to feel like we can truly be ourselves and be accepted for who we are by the people closest to us. Being our authentic selves means our thoughts, words, and actions closely align with our values, beliefs, and intentions. Authenticity isn't about sharing everything; it's about freedom from burying or disguising parts of ourselves. How authentic we each feel we can be with one another serves as a key indicator of the health of our relationship.

To be authentic, we need to understand ourselves (self-awareness), communicate truthfully (honesty), and take the necessary risks to express who we are (vulnerability). For the formula lovers out there, you can think of authenticity this way:

SELF-AWARENESS + HONESTY + VULNERABILITY = AUTHENTICITY

Let's explore these three elements in more depth.

Self-Awareness

Self-awareness is the foundation of the authenticity equation—and make no mistake, it is an ongoing journey. We may never fully understand *everything* about ourselves, but pursuing that understanding is what allows us to be intentional with how we grow. In the previous chapter, we established the importance of curiosity. Self-awareness requires curious self-reflection and focused introspection around the parts of us we're most self-critical about and the parts still unknown to us. This is where authenticity starts: putting in the work to get to know yourself.

This means we need to go beyond who we think we *should* be, how we think we *should* act, and who we think other people *want* us to be. We need to be able to differentiate what we think, feel, and believe from what others think, feel, and believe. As author of *Good Inside*, Dr. Becky Kennedy, points out, a parent's voice becomes a child's self-talk.[1] And it isn't only our parents whose words influence our internal world. Whether it's the tone of harsh criticism from a coach, the way your drama teacher gives praise, or general cultural influences, they all have the power to permeate our inner voice. When we notice the other influences as separate and get familiar with our true internal voice, we can find deeper self-awareness.

Whether it's through journaling, therapy, a book club, or deep conversations with a good friend, make sure you are investing in your self-awareness. Notice that only one of these activities is a solitary activity. Although self-awareness requires curiosity about *yourself*, it's often best achieved through the help and support of trusted relationships. Other people can be our best mirrors (especially when we struggle to see a piece of ourselves) and provide the spark for self-inquiry. So don't think that self-awareness has to be a solitary journey—in fact, it shouldn't be!

Self-awareness lays the groundwork to better facilitate the other two components of authenticity. It allows us to understand our truth so that we can better communicate it. We can only stand confidently in our truth and have clarity on which risks are worth taking once we know ourselves.

Put simply, we cannot be true to ourselves if we do not yet know who we are.

Honesty

When you sense authenticity in someone, part of that feeling often comes from the sense that they are straightforward, that they are telling the truth (or at least their truth). Conversely, an inauthentic person has an air of artificiality about them, as if they're pretending to be someone they are not, or they're outright lying.

Whether in school or the office, many of us have witnessed or been part of the following scenario:

Stacey presents a proposal she worked hard on. Amber goes up to her and says, "Great proposal! I loved it. I think the executive team will choose it."

Minutes or hours later you see Amber tap on Luna's shoulder and lean in to say, "Did you see Stacey's proposal? How basic and uninventive; a second grader could have come up with that," as she laughs, makes a face, and walks away.

In such situations, it doesn't even matter which of Amber's statements represents her true opinion, her contradictory statements demonstrate dishonesty.

To help people trust us and feel safe around us, we must be honest with them. And to be authentic, we also need to be honest with ourselves. To stay rooted in authenticity requires consistent honesty, which can be a scary thing—especially if you're someone who highly values approval from others.

Simply put, we cannot be true to ourselves if we aren't truthful.

Vulnerability

Honesty is easy enough when your opinion doesn't go against the grain or when you only have positive feedback to give. But when the topic of conversation gets harder, it takes real courage to be your full and honest self.

Vulnerability is essential to authenticity because it takes self-awareness and honesty to the next level. As Brené Brown defines it, vulnerability is "the emotion that we experience during times of uncertainty, risk, and emotional exposure."[2] While life is full of uncertainty, risk, and emotional exposure, certain relationships and environments have more than others.

In a group with a rigid "our way is the only way" mentality, where judgment is high, it is far riskier to be honest. In environments like these, being different takes more courage and requires vulnerability.

For example, imagine you were born and raised within a family of artists. Your whole life, you've been surrounded by adults lamenting the monotonous lives of "boring academic types" and the "drones" of society. If you want to become a painter, sharing this with your family of artists doesn't pose much of a risk. If your sibling covets a PhD in advanced chemistry, on the other hand, it will require vulnerability to ask for support in this kind of family.

It is no more or less authentic for either of you to share your career aspirations, but if your dreams align with your family's established values, it takes less risk to be authentic. It is in these moments, when emotional exposure is especially risky, that we are called to lean into vulnerability, which is always easier said than done. To some extent, all human interaction involves uncertainty and risk. We are hardwired to avoid rejection, and emotional exposure is putting our woundable selves out there to potentially be judged, ridiculed, and even exiled, which is why authenticity can feel particularly challenging. After all, authenticity is about knowing who you are at your core and being true to that core self, even when you feel the risk of rejection.

Connection: Belonging Versus Fitting In

A sense of belonging is a fundamental human need.

Brené Brown describes connection as "the energy that exists between people when they feel seen, heard, and valued." Despite our best efforts to bend and break ourselves to find connection in our hope for belonging, Brown reminds us that "true belonging doesn't require us to change who we are; it requires us to be who we are."[3]

Belonging: a deep sense of interconnectedness with those around us based on our true selves

Fitting in: conforming to meet the expectations of others—trying to put our star-shaped self into a square box

If our fear of rejection or judgment prevents us from being wholly authentic, we may *fit in*, but we will feel even more alone because we won't truly *belong*. We will know, deep down, that we haven't shown people who we really are. While they may love and accept what they see, that love and acceptance will be for a false version of us. Any approval we receive while being inauthentic can subsequently make us feel even more alienated and confirm a deep internal fear that our authentic selves would never be accepted, let alone valued.

Although it might feel better to think of fitting in as a step toward belonging, the truth is that it actively prevents us from belonging with others, and more importantly, it keeps us from feeling a sense of belonging to ourselves. We must be brave and show up authentically if we hope to belong.

Imagine you've just joined a new company. You had a rough job search and are really excited but incredibly nervous to get off to the right start. On day one, your whole team is chatting about their shared love and fandom of the Red Sox. You aren't shocked—the company is based in Boston—but as a Yankees fan you have a hard decision to make. You grew up in New York, and your favorite childhood memories are when your late grandfather took you into the city for Yankees games. You didn't even like baseball, but the long drive down from your small town up north was full of the best conversations, and now you associate the Yankees with him.

Fitting in says stay quiet, smile, and go along with the team-wide Red Sox fandom. Belonging says be vulnerably you.

If you pretend to like the Red Sox, you might get invited to a viewing party and feel instantly part of the in crowd. But you may always wonder if they only like you because of a shared sports team.

If you share the cherished trips you took with your grandfather and his influence on your favorite team, you might just find out a few others deeply miss a beloved grandparent too, even if they give you a hard time for being a Yankees fan. Your vulnerability provides the opportunity for Alok from accounting to learn something about you that inspires them to invite you to lunch. At lunch they let you know they have fond memories of driving up to the area you grew up for summer holidays. Over the meal, you develop an authentic connection.

Authenticity offers the opportunity to find your people and a grounded sense of belonging.

Authenticity and Intuition

Paradoxically, when we most want to fit in and try so hard (inauthentically) to fit in, others sense it. (That's a big part of why middle school can be so hard.) As a protection mechanism, human beings have developed a keen radar to detect when people are authentic versus inauthentic or, even worse, intentionally deceptive. From our earliest years, we develop and hone our ability to observe tone of voice, body language, and context clues to evaluate those around us for signs of trustworthiness. When we intuit that someone is hiding something from us, we innately question whether we can trust them, which can often show up as a physical sensation or a gut feeling.

Let's look at a common example of how this can play out in the workplace:

Marta is the manager of her company's PR team. She's always felt like a fair and honest manager, but she was disappointed and frustrated during her annual review last December when she received feedback that she is too negative and critical of her employees. To shift this perception, she's decided that this year, even when she's unimpressed with a deliverable, she'll try to find something nice to say.

Collin is a designer on Marta's team. During the team's biggest project last year, he spent a considerable amount of time developing custom graphics for the campaign. He felt good about his work, and the rest of the team seemed really impressed. However, the minute Marta saw the graphics, her face turned sour. "Did you get these from some free website?" she asked. "They feel too cheap and cartoony for the brand persona." Collin was devastated.

Now, as he wraps up version one of the first project of the year, Collin cautiously awaits Marta's feedback. She calls him into her office and starts by saying, "I like the color scheme you used on this graphic!" But unfortunately, Marta's face betrays her message. While her words may sound nice, her expression is once again sour—an expression Collin knows all too well. Collin can feel her insincerity, which is even worse than just hearing painful (but authentic) feedback.

A few months later, when Marta receives her new performance review, it indicates that she is not only negative and critical but also phony. Now Marta is angry. She has actively made changes to her behavior, and it hasn't worked.

Simply changing our behavior, without understanding and addressing what's behind it, will often come off as inauthentic and can damage relationships. Marta's mistake wasn't saying nice things during feedback but saying them despite an overwhelming feeling of disappointment, muzzling her true thoughts. After Marta received last year's initial feedback about being too harsh, if she had handled it authentically, here's what she could've said to her team:

Hey, team, I recognize that my approach hasn't been working, and I want to do better. I know I can be a bit of a perfectionist. I tend to be overly ambitious, and I often get caught up in focusing only on what we can improve. I can be overly sarcastic, especially when I'm nervous or tired, and I appreciate it can come across as meaner than I intend. I understand that it's also important to celebrate progress and call out what is right, and I want to get better at doing so before speaking to what needs to ~et better. I clearly don't say it enough, but you all do great work. I know I often get hyperspecific about the tiniest detail I don't like, which can be discouraging. You are all such talented designers—and I haven't done a good job of making that abundantly clear. Since this isn't easy for me, I know I'll make mistakes along the way, but I will try my best. And if I ever fall back into my old habits with feedback, please tell me in the moment so I can learn to better catch myself.

Had Marta said something like this once she made the decision to improve her feedback delivery, her team would have more likely felt heard and thus been more content with her response. Collin and his colleagues might've given her some grace as she critiqued their work. "What do you like about this?" they may have asked, as a gentle reminder to acknowledge the good parts and focus on improving in each iteration.

Notice that in the example above, we don't approach authenticity as Marta thinking to herself, *Hey, I'm a perfectionist, and if people don't like it, that's their problem. They'll just have to deal with it. I'm the boss, and this is who I am.* Authenticity is not an excuse to treat people poorly, to utter any thought that enters your mind, or to give up on growing and improving. Authenticity isn't about acting out your every whim and desire or disregarding your impact on others. In fact, treating people poorly and speaking without a filter when you're upset is simply emotional dysregulation.

While being hurt or upset when receiving bad feedback is fine and authentic to feel or share, reacting meanly out of spite or defensiveness underlines your inability to handle the emotion. When we are exhausted and don't feel seen or understood, we may express frustration in emotionally dysregulated outbursts we are not proud of moments later. We don't need to suppress or hide our authentic selves to coexist in this world, but we absolutely need to learn how to emotionally regulate to avoid such moments and practice repair after an emotionally driven reaction we aren't proud of.

Learning to fully understand and communicate how we feel is an empowering endeavor. Emotional literacy and regulation will help each of us, and our team as a whole, in the long term. When we take the time to normalize human emotions and learn to express ourselves mindfully, we become authentic communicators. Only when we can feel our emotions, learn to identify and express them, and be courageous and authentic with ourselves and others can we find true connection.

Authenticity is more than emotionally regulated self-expression; it's the foundation of trust, belonging, and strong leadership. The more we get to know ourselves, the more honest we are with ourselves and one another, and the more we embrace vulnerability, the more we empower those around us to do the same.

INVITING FEEDBACK

Marta didn't show up curious and seek to understand the feedback of her employees in order to adjust her behavior authentically. Instead, she tried to improve her reviews through inauthentic behavior changes. Not embracing self-awareness, honesty, and vulnerability prevented her from important insights that would have helped her, the entire team, and ultimately, their work product. We must work on how to be receptive and implement feedback if we hope to have an authentic culture. When a team member is willing to offer tough feedback to a person in a position of authority, they are demonstrating courage and vulnerability. We may not always agree with the feedback, and that's okay. But we must be at the very least open to hearing it and taking it into account.

As leaders, if we respond by arguing, criticizing, threatening their position, or jeopardizing their potential for a promotion, we demonstrate that it is not safe to be courageous and vulnerable. Or if we cut them off, disengage, or pay lip service but ultimately ignore the issue after they've invested time and energy into providing something of use, we're telling them it isn't worth our time. Nothing comes from their effort.

Your receptiveness to others' feedback signals your level of commitment to improvement to the group. If you expect other people to take your feedback but never expect to receive difficult feedback yourself, you'll be rightfully seen as a hypocrite and lose credibility as someone interested in growing and learning. When this is the tone we set, we discourage honesty and, subsequently, authenticity.

Alternatively, leaders who not only seek constructive feedback regularly but also genuinely listen to and act on that feedback signal to the team that feedback and growth are expected from everyone. And it's crucial that we respond positively to constructive feedback. Here are some examples of what that can sound like:

- Thank you for letting me know. I wasn't aware I was showing up like that.
- This is super helpful information. I really appreciate you bringing it to me.
- Do you mind if we come up with a game plan together for how I can start working on this now?

It's important to keep in mind that, as leaders, we're not just reacting to feedback as ourselves in a given moment but rather modeling the way we'd like feedback to be received by everyone on the team. If we wouldn't like someone to respond defensively or get worked up when we give them difficult feedback, we need to act accordingly when it's our turn. This encourages honesty from the team in the same way that defensive responses to negative feedback discourage it.

Cultivating a Culture of Authenticity

As leaders, we can ensure our team of Sox lovers are inclusive to non-Sox fans and the baseball-indifferent population alike. How do we start?

At a team level, self-awareness for leaders is about knowing where your people are at, who they are as individuals, and who they become as a group. While assessments and surveys can help inform what's behind interpersonal and team dynamics, investing time to get to know your people is essential. Honesty is perhaps the easiest to translate. The truth matters whether it's spoken to one another privately or in front of the whole team. For many of us, vulnerability feels significantly harder in large groups, so when leaders model vulnerability and set expectations of how to show up for and support one another, it helps. This can look like clear rules about honesty and reinforcing that it's safe to be vulnerable. Ultimately, the goal of a culture of authenticity is to empower people to bring their whole selves to work.

As leaders, we can cultivate a workplace environment where it feels less risky and more valuable to take the risk of being vulnerable. In his book *Speak-Up Culture*, our friend and colleague

Stephen Shedletzky describes a speak-up culture as one in which "people feel it is both safe and worth it to share their ideas, concerns, disagreements and mistakes without fear of being ignored or punished."[4] This is an ideal description of an environment in which authenticity can thrive and spread. Don't wait for this to happen. Leaders are the ones who set the tone and have the biggest effect. Authenticity goes beyond what we say. Much of our authentic expression is nonverbal, from how we dress or style ourselves to our hobbies, rituals, belief systems, and even cherished holidays.

If a leader models authenticity and encourages and celebrates authenticity in others, the odds are higher that individuals will embrace authenticity, and the team will thrive. On the other hand, if a leader teases people when they're being vulnerable, retaliates against them when they share honest, negative feedback, or even just allows others to do so, authenticity across the team will decrease. It really is up to the leader to encourage and reward people for sharing their truth and making the environment both safe and encouraging for employees to speak up and show up authentically.

We can design our workplaces to celebrate and uplift diverse voices by inviting respectful disagreement, especially from traditionally marginalized voices, even—and often most importantly— when it makes us uncomfortable. Whether you opt to acknowledge diverse holidays or no holidays at all, for example, ensure that you do so consistently and in a way that is aligned with how you want people to feel and show up.

Here's how one team might set the stage for authentic collaboration:

- All opinions are welcome—good, bad, or ugly—but homophobia, racism, and other prejudices are not permitted.

- We challenge one another's ideas, assumptions, and opinions; we do not demean people.
- Raised voices are fine; pointed accusations are not.
- Yelling is okay. Singing is better. Laughter is a must.

A different creative team might require a different approach to encourage authenticity:

- We write our ideas first and place them anonymously into a bowl.
- Zen only. We are collecting ideas. There is no right answer.
- After reading the ideas, we have one minute of quiet reflection.
- The facilitator reads each idea aloud, and we reply with statements and questions that start with "Yes, and . . ."

With intention, we can build environments that embolden our teams to be brave and vulnerable. As leaders, we have the power to make or break the threshold for authenticity.

This might look like:

- Admitting that you don't know the answer, but you will do your best to find it
- Building relationships with your people by participating in a March Madness fantasy basketball league—joyously expressing your sporty competitive side
- Acknowledging when you are scared, feel overwhelmed, or need help—even if it's just to another executive, a trusted mentor, or one of your direct reports

There is no shortcut to authenticity. You cannot copy-paste or mirror someone else's authentic expression and expect it to feel genuine. Discomfort with any level of vulnerability is normal, especially in the beginning. Over time and with practice, however, grounded confidence in your authentic expression will grow, and connections with your team will deepen.

What Gets in the Way

FEAR OF DISAPPOINTING PEOPLE

When those we look up to disapprove of who we are—whether the judgment is rooted in religious, national, cultural, or other belief systems—fear of disappointing them is a powerful motivator to hide parts of ourselves. This fear is especially prominent in highly homogenous environments and can be paralyzing when we think about showing up authentically.

FEAR OF TAKING UP TOO MUCH SPACE

For many—especially those in marginalized communities—the idea of showing up in an authentic way carries a sense of guilt, worry, or shame. This fear of taking up space often leads to prioritizing the desires of others above our own authentic needs. For example, many women have been taught to be as small and agreeable as possible, both literally and figuratively. And when they step outside of these narrow conventions, they are made to feel wrong for not abiding by the "rules." It is the challenge of a lifetime to feel confident holding space in a world that wasn't built for us, which can put a firm stranglehold on our ability to stand in our authenticity.

FEAR OF RETALIATION

As we discussed in the section on vulnerability, some truths are riskier than others. It is one thing to disagree with a more tenured colleague's taste in music. It is entirely different to share personal details that in the wrong hands could lead to discrimination, loss of livelihood, or physical harm. Music disagreements might lead to ridicule, which, while still unpleasant, doesn't usually have severe consequences. Retaliation, on the other hand, can have life-altering consequences such as demotion, exclusion from promotions or bonuses, or even termination. If that's at stake in your team, there is no chance for authentic expression.

Practice Makes Progress

INDIVIDUAL PRACTICES

Get to Know More of Yourself

Often, our own self-perception is inaccurate or, at the very least, incomplete. We experience the world—and even ourselves—through the lens of our own biases. To gain a less biased account of our natural skills and strengths, we can use strengths assessments like CliftonStrengths, Enneagram, DISC, or the one by our friend Rich Diviney, author of *The Attributes*, who has a great assessment for understanding yourself and your improvement areas. Having others—whether colleagues, friends, or family members—hold up a mirror to us is important. We all have blind spots, and just like rearview mirrors reveal blind spots on the road, other people can reveal them in our own lives.

A mirror's job is not to define our self-talk or unique perspective but rather to help us see ourselves from different angles. Seek out people who can help you with the angles that you may struggle to see. While staying open to other perspectives, practice discernment. The ultimate goal is to strengthen your inner clarity and trust in yourself.

Create Reminders

Whether it's a calendar event, a sticky note, or a framed print by your desk, pick something that motivates and reminds you to stay authentic. For some, the risk of disappointing others compels them to show up in inauthentic ways. These folks might benefit from a notification five minutes before a meeting with senior leaders which simply reads Tell Your Truth. Others may benefit from a sticky note on their computer monitor or mirror that reminds them to check in with themselves throughout the day by asking something like, "What do I genuinely want, need, think, or feel right now?" Whatever method you choose, make sure it's something you'll see every day.

Introduce Your View Your Way

Speaking your truth can be hard, especially when you are afraid of what the consequences might be for having a contrary opinion. For those who are nonconfrontational or have people-pleasing tendencies, it can feel almost impossible. If you're one of these people, finding a way to introduce your view can make all the difference. Rather than saying things like, "No way," "You're wrong," or "I disagree," try sharing your thoughts through phrases like these:

- Can I offer another perspective?
- I want to get on the same page. Something I'm struggling with about this is _____.
- I hadn't thought of it that way. Do you mind if I share my experience of it?

These phrases honor the other's perspective and introduce space for your own in a respectful way. When we speak up in a way that honors differing points of view, we make tension and conflict more generative than divisive. Finding your own way of doing it will take practice and experimentation, but it pays dividends in the long term. No matter what you choose to say, focus on creating alignment and understanding versus making one person right or wrong.

TEAM-WIDE PRACTICES

Expand Self-Learning

It's one thing to get to know yourself better so that you can improve. However, imagine the power of a team that is not only self-aware but also shares their learnings with their teammates! Going through assessments, like those mentioned above, as a group allows us to (1) learn about our own strengths, passions, and areas for improvement; (2) learn about our teammates' strengths, passions, and areas for improvement; and (3) set the team on a learning and growing path together. For lasting impact and team-wide effects, it's essential to build a plan for how to utilize this information. Incorporate it into your one-on-ones as a check-in tool. Integrate it into the team's learning and development curriculum. Take different assessments and discuss what each team member learned from each experience. Have conversations as a team about how you can utilize each member's unique strengths, passions, and interests to better communicate and collaborate. Set the expectation with the team that learning more about ourselves is a constant journey that we are all on together.

Invite the Missing Perspective

When exploring a new potential pathway or decision, it's natural to consider outside perspectives. For example, you may ask yourself questions like, "What might the customer think?" Asking similar questions within our teams can also be a great idea and will encourage more authenticity. When engaging in a subject where alignment seems to be high, it can be useful to ask a question like, "What perspective might we be missing right now?" or "What are some reasonable alternatives to _____?" By asking these questions, we are encouraging people to bring different ideas forth during discussion. Standing out against the crowd can be a scary thing, especially when your boss is part of that crowd. Putting forth a prompt like this gives people the opportunity to share differing perspectives that they may or may not hold themselves, in a nonconfrontational way. The more confidence we can give our team members when they take risks speaking up, the more authenticity we promote.

Combat Gossip

Create psychological safety by supporting self-awareness, honesty, and vulnerability from your team members. This requires transparent dialogue and open communication to encourage direct conversations instead of gossip or siloed conversations, which tend to keep information hidden from the larger group and exclusive to a select few. A culture of gossip tells people that if they step out of line with what some people want, they will be ridiculed or even punished. Few things will stifle authenticity quicker than the risk of public humiliation. Mitigating this risk looks like addressing rumors out loud as a team. Here's an example of what a leader might say:

Hey, team, I know Sally is offline this week, and I've heard a few people theorizing and trying to figure out why she's gone. On this team, we either directly ask the person, or we go to someone who might know. We don't just gossip. So what I can share is that Sally is offline for a family health situation. Beyond that, I'd appreciate it if we all respect her privacy, and if anyone has any questions about how this affects your work or projects, please ask Tim.

AUTHENTICITY SNAPSHOT 📷

OUR DEFINITION

Authenticity is showing up as your truest self—the intersection of self-awareness, honesty, and vulnerability.

Self-Awareness + Honesty + Vulnerability = Authenticity

KEY TAKEAWAYS

- Authenticity requires self-awareness, honesty, and vulnerability, which work together to help us connect with and express our truest selves.
- Self-awareness helps us separate our authentic voice from external influences.
- Our self-awareness is enhanced by seeking perspectives from trusted relationships.
- Honesty—with ourselves and others—is essential to creating trust and fostering authentic connections.
- Vulnerability, the courage to be our truest selves, is a risk we must take to embody authenticity.
- To cultivate a work environment where it feels less risky to be honest and vulnerable, leaders must model authenticity and encourage and celebrate it in others.

WHAT GETS IN THE WAY

- Fear of disappointing people
- Fear of taking up too much space
- Fear of retaliation

PRACTICE MAKES PROGRESS

- **Individual Practices**
  - Get to know more of yourself.
  - Create reminders.
  - Introduce your view your way.

- **Team-Wide Practices**
  - Expand self-learning.
  - Invite the missing perspective.
  - Combat gossip.

CHAPTER 6

Embodiment #3: Care

*Too often, we underestimate the power of a touch, a smile, a kind
word, a listening ear, an honest compliment, or the smallest act
of caring, all of which have the potential to turn a life around.*
—**Leo Buscaglia**

**Care is showing up in service of someone in a way that
demonstrates that you value them enough to invest in
their well-being, even when it isn't easy or convenient.**

While care can be a general sentiment of concern, there's more to it than that. How often do we hear people say they care about something without taking meaningful action toward protecting it? It's common to hear people espouse they care about a group of people, be it their employees or the factory workers at their supplier; but there is a big difference between caring *about* and caring *for*. To embody genuine care, we must act with intention and show up in service of whom or what we care about.

Think about a person in your life who cares about you. Just thinking about that person likely gives you a warm feeling. They've demonstrated how much they care through their behaviors and actions toward you over time. Maybe they offered to drive an hour across town during rush hour to pick you up from the airport, just so you'd be welcomed by a familiar face. Or perhaps when you were recovering from a particularly bad flu, they dropped off your favorite soup. They don't just say they care about you; they actually care *for* you.

Our team led a workshop recently for a group of senior executives and took them through a session on care. During this session, we asked them to get into small groups and share a time that they felt cared for. Not one person mentioned receiving congratulations after a big win or promotion. Nor did they discuss getting a polite "you've got this" type of platitude. Not even one mentioned getting a bonus. Every story the executives shared had to do with someone who understood what was going on in their life and took the time to check in on them or offer support during a challenging time. Each time we show up for someone during these moments is an opportunity for connection.

Showing up in service of someone begins with getting to know them, leveraging curiosity and then authenticity to deepen your connection. This is the reason that care comes after curiosity and authenticity. Often the most meaningful moments of care show someone that you know them. By showing up curious and having authentic conversations, we get to know each other on a deeper level. To invest in someone's well-being in an impactful way, we first must learn what they actually want and need.

Getting to know someone well enough to have a better idea of those wants and needs—and to have a relationship where you can ask, "How can I best support you right now?"—takes time and investment. As we learn more, we improve the probability of making meaningful impact, even through the smallest of gestures. That intentional effort is an important distinction of something that is often confused with, but can get in the way of, care: being nice.

Care ≠ Nice

It's common to conflate the two concepts, and many caring behaviors do feel nice. Care sometimes can look like listening to someone in a time of need, giving an occasional token of appreciation, sharing opportunities for advancement, or taking dietary preferences into consideration for the company cookout. Challenging moments often present important opportunities to show up in service, such as the need for a hard conversation, offering comfort during a tough time, providing honest advice when someone asks for it, and empathizing with a colleague struggling to handle a new schedule. These opportunities call for embracing discomfort to demonstrate care.

The difference between care and niceness is rooted in intention. Niceness is about politeness and professionalism (i.e., appearances). Being nice is fine and often even called for, especially if it's a simple interaction and you're not aiming to strengthen your relationship with that person. Yet, nice is dangerous when it dictates doing the opposite of what someone needs. When, for example, the nice thing to do is to politely sidestep a sensitive topic, which may leave them feeling alone.

In these challenging moments, caring is often harder. It can be awkward, and it can require showing softness and emotion, which many of us struggle with, especially in modern professional environments. It starts early. As young children, we're taught to be *nice*. As young adults, we're expected to be *polite*. And the expectation carries over into adulthood when we enter the workforce and learn to exhibit *professionalism*. Let's look at an example:

Imagine that Bob, your colleague at work, is going through a hard time. His spouse has been diagnosed with terminal cancer and is undergoing chemotherapy. The nice, polite, professional thing to do is smile and not directly address Bob's hardship, or perhaps share platitudes:

This too shall pass. Hang in there. Tomorrow will be better.

Nice, polite professionalism says not to ask Bob how he and his spouse are doing, as that may lead to discomfort or an outward display of negative, potentially mushy emotions.

If you've taken the time to get curious about Bob and have built a relationship where you both show up authentically, you might already know that he'd appreciate a private conversation rather than trying to force a brave face in front of other colleagues. This being the case, caring can look like skipping the public platitudes, leaving a short note on Bob's desk inviting him to grab coffee at his favorite café, and showing up to listen and hold space for him when he's ready.

Your insight to what type of support Bob needs and prefers helped you avoid the pitfall of shining a light on his suffering and making him uncomfortable in a group setting. The more we know about a person and learn what's most meaningful to them, the better we can authentically show up in service of their current and future well-being.

You might think the example with Bob is a bit extreme and something you won't encounter in your career. We certainly hope the people around you don't suffer a life event like Bob's, though it's inevitable that each of us will experience difficulties throughout our lives. While we all prefer to celebrate joyous times together, the call for care shows up most often during tough times. It can be messy, inconveniently timed, and involve unpleasant emotions. This is even true when we demonstrate care through challenges on a much smaller scale than Bob's example, like when a colleague misses the company picnic because they woke up to a flooded basement, or their daughter broke her ankle and is stuck in a cast. Showing up in service of people during these times, big or small, strengthens the bonds between us.

Cultivating a Culture of Care

As a leader, opportunities to show your team and colleagues that you care about them abound. It shouldn't be a surprise by now that our first recommendation when scaling care in your workplace is to start by focusing on how you show up and embody care. When a leader checks in on how we're doing, takes a genuine interest in our well-being and growth, and supports us through ups and downs, it has far-reaching implications. The relationships we have with our direct leaders and colleagues impact how we perform on the job, how much work we miss, how long we stay with an employer, and even our physical health and lifespan.

While shifting toward caring for others in one-on-one interactions is an important step to cultivating a culture of care across your team and organization, sustainable team-wide care requires systems. This is where care-centric policies and practices come into play. Many companies out there are happy to boast about such policies in their recruiting materials. Unlimited PTO. Free gym memberships. On-site yoga. It all sounds great. But when the time comes to actually use these perks, many of us are met with resistance.

We've all experienced the difference between what is said and what is done. Saying your people's well-being matters without demonstrating it won't work. When our stated policies don't match how we actually behave, culture follows the observable behaviors, not the idealistic words on a website or wall.

For example, many of us have had bosses say, "If you're sick, take time off. That's why we have unlimited PTO!" But when we finally did, it was held against us. So, naturally, it's hard to trust vague, generous PTO policies or a new manager that tells you to take the sick time you need.

Cultural context and lived experience matter. Which is why, if such a policy exists on your team, it isn't enough to say it. As the leader, you have to operationalize the boundaries that protect the values you espouse. Beyond saying, "Take care of yourself—health is a priority," you have to model the behavior, empower others to do so, celebrate when people take time, and even send someone home when they don't. This might require you pulling rank when you see a teammate trying to tough it out.

Imagine this scenario: After checking in with Todd on how he feels, hearing how sick he is, and telling him he can take time off, he still insists he doesn't need it. This is when it's time to operationalize your values with a clear boundary: "Todd, you are clearly sick. On this team we value health. I need you to log off. Your well-being is more important than the tasks you are working on." For the most time-sensitive tasks on his plate, do your best to cover, delegate, or let relevant people know there will be a delay in response, and if something does fall through the cracks, or someone asks why a task assigned to Todd didn't get done, have his back.

Care-centric benefits aren't about writing something that sounds good in theory. They don't follow trends like unlimited PTO to "keep up" or simply attract talent; they build intentional support systems into their operating procedures. In the case of unlimited PTO to be used as sick time and vacation, this might look like having enough staff and resources to cover each other without flooding anyone to empower people to take the time they need. Balanced workloads, a simple process for requesting sick time, and transparency with all shareholders that caring for employee well-being influences your operations—all set up Todd to take the sick time he needs to return refreshed and ready to show up in service of the rest of the team and clients.

Build in the expectation that all employees should take the time they need and prioritize their well-being—then model it and normalize it. This takes the burden and pressure off individuals, who might worry that their using sick time will overburden their colleagues, upset their clients, or delay workflows.

While prioritizing health with unlimited PTO for sick time is a specific example of a value that demonstrates care, the lesson is true across the board. To ensure you aren't just saying you care but are actually caring for your people, make sure that whatever care-centric benefits you offer are accessible! Whether it's taking vacation time or utilizing your learning and development budget to buy a course, driving a caring culture that positively impacts your company requires a willingness to operationalize your care-focused values and stand by them.

Once we're able to set the tone for how we expect our teammates to care for one another, we begin to normalize this behavior, and it becomes part of the culture. Additionally, when we prioritize creating the space for and expectation of care across the team through implementing personal and team-wide care practices, the work of caring is shared. As a leader, you need to get the ball rolling. Once it becomes ingrained in the team's DNA, teammates will check and support one another through ups and downs.

When we live our values out loud, especially when we show up in service of our people, we create a workplace where we shift from surviving to thriving. Embodied care is a direct signal to your team that they matter beyond mere transactions or outputs and emphasizes the *human* in human-focused workplaces. The most impactful leaders are not the ones who demand the most from their teams; they are the ones who invest in their people becoming the best possible versions of themselves.

What Gets in the Way

THE STORIES WE TELL OURSELVES

Through our experiences growing up and notable situations or relationships, we all accept certain ideas as truth or "just the way things are." These inform our internal narrative and the stories we tell ourselves. Often, even without realizing it, these stories lead us to shut ourselves off from trying to reach out, connect, or offer care.

If one of the stories we tell ourselves is our colleague doesn't want us to bring up their missing wedding band, it will often prevent us from expressing just how much we notice them and care how they are doing.

Additionally, there are cases when someone offers a caring gesture, and the stories you tell yourself prevent you from accepting it. If you believe that accepting would make you a burden, you're unlikely to accept. When you don't want to take up their time or energy, or associate needing help with feeling guilt or shame, you'll avoid asking for what you need. If we tell ourselves we are a bother, we can stop ourselves from showing care and deprive others of the opportunity to care for us.

TIME SCARCITY

The narrative that caring for others is a drain on your time is probably the single most common refrain we hear, not only from corporate leaders but also from parents, students, and everyone in between. *Who has time?!* And indeed, showing up for the people around you can and should take up a decent amount of your time. It's true that time is a finite resource, and when we are busy people, it is a scarce one. So, if we don't see relationships as a top priority, it's easy for us to prioritize tons of other things. We can end up never taking the time to get to know and care for others.

HYPERCOMPETITIVE WORKPLACES

A lot of organizations actively encourage employees to look out only for themselves. Imagine a team where sales folks earn a too-low-to-survive base salary. Now picture a boss who flames internal competition for the limited bonuses and only offers incentive structures focused on outperforming colleagues in rankings. In such an environment, it can seem like or even literally become a zero-sum game. Naturally, employees can slip into seeing their coworkers not just as competition but also as obstacles to their personal success and their financial survival.

A QUID PRO QUO MENTALITY

While self-interest is inevitable, if we are too focused on our wants, needs, desires, goals, and perceptions, our self-interest can become a blocker. We see this play out when people try to justify a lack of caring by saying things like, "What about what's on my plate? What do I get out of trying to take on theirs too?" When we expect to get something in exchange for demonstrating even a simple kindness or a caring for someone, there's no space to embody care. This is especially prevalent in highly competitive workspaces like the one described above.

A "YOU GO FIRST" MENTALITY

Some people justify a lack of caring by looking at service as a transaction, similar to those with a quid pro quo mentality. However, they might say things like, "Nobody cared when I was going through some personal issues. Why should I care about so-and-so?" The implication being that they should only show up for other people once they've already received a similar level of care themselves. When the story we tell ourselves is that others are indifferent toward us, it can be much harder to find the motivation to show up for them. After all, it's easier for us to care for others when we feel cared for by them. However, if we all wait to show up for others until someone else does it for us first, no one ever shows up.

OUTDATED IDEAS OF STRENGTH

People widely associate leadership with projecting strength. Some even say that the only way to accomplish that is to leverage power over others, that you must know it all, and you should be superhuman if you want to be a strong leader. And many of us grew up in cultures that reinforced a common misconception that when someone demonstrates care for the people around them, they look weak or soft. When we limit our idea of strength to these misguided notions, we perpetuate antiquated tropes that shut down care.

Practice Makes Progress

INDIVIDUAL PRACTICES

Block Out Time for Connection

If you have a say in how you spend your time at work, block off time every single week to check in with your colleagues. You can accomplish this in various ways. If you're in the office, this might look like walking the floor, asking how people are doing, and stopping by your employees' desks to check in. Or perhaps you want to be more intentional about who you meet with and when. If so, book check-in meetings with specific team members. Maybe go for a walk together or do something to get off campus for a while and more naturally shed formality. For remote teams, this can look like sending Slack messages to folks you haven't had a one-on-one with this week or following up with someone who's experiencing a challenging time. Even if your workday doesn't have a lot of flexibility, you can take advantage of your breaks and lunch to connect with teammates. Whatever you do, make sure you're proactively dedicating time every week and not just giving your team members the scraps of what little (i.e., zero) leftover time you have.

Get to Know Someone Better

You can't schedule when someone is going to need care. All we can do as leaders is prepare as much as we can in advance so that when the time comes, we are ready to show up for one another. As our dentists and doctors love to remind us, it's better to stay on top of our health through daily maintenance than to wait until disaster strikes. The same is true for identifying the best ways to care for people. This week—and maybe every week—pick a person on your team to spend extra time with and get to know them on a deeper level. When we take time to connect with someone and understand them more deeply, it will put us in a better position to care for them in a meaningful way when they need it most.

Check Your Intentions

Remember, niceness ≠ care. It's hard not to engage our niceness autopilot when someone is struggling. This is especially true when we are in a hurry or don't have high energy levels to engage with people. It may be tempting to throw out the classic pleasantries, especially when the idea of sitting with that person's emotions makes you uncomfortable. When you are interested in building warm connections and deeper relationships, though, it is important to be intentionally caring. If you want to know how someone is doing, make the time to ask them genuinely and allow time for their whole answer. You don't have to be able to fix anything for them. Just offer them the opportunity to feel heard.

TEAM-WIDE PRACTICES

Create an Expectation of Connection

Being vulnerable with people we don't know very well is tough. It's easier to be ourselves with people we already trust. And building that kind of trust takes time and getting to know one another beyond roles and work personas. Sure, you may meet with everyone on the team for one-on-ones if you're the manager, but how often do teammates get one-on-one time with each other? Set the expectation that teammates need to meet regularly to connect and learn more about the humans they work with. There are tons of great tools and apps that can help with this. For example, if your team uses Slack, there's an app called Donut that facilitates invites for people to organize one-on-one coffee breaks (in person or virtual). Whether it's cross-team or org-wide, weekly or monthly, set it up and be clear about expectations!

Budget for Care Surprises

Whether for each other or for clients, budgeting for tokens of care—such as a handwritten card, a cup of coffee, or a custom-decorated tote bag—enables folks to show care in impactful ways. It doesn't need to be a huge dollar amount, but making sure that employees have some dedicated time and money to show others that they are valued communicates clearly that this is important to the team and the organization. Expecting people to use their own time and money for these things all but ensures that it won't become a common practice.

Align Behavior with Systems

Benefits packages that include generous PTO, unlimited vacation time, and large learning and development budgets alone can fall short. As James Clear says, "You do not rise to the level of your goals. You fall to the level of your systems."[1] As leaders, it's our job to implement systems that give employees clear, unobstructed access to opportunities and resources that invest in their well-being, so they can feel confident in utilizing these policies.

This means that if care-centric policies and benefits packages don't exist, create them. When you have such policies, your reactions to people's use of them determines if and how much people use them moving forward.

Guilting or shaming people for making use of a company policy, resource, or benefit undermines employee well-being. Additionally, when an employee isn't leveraging these tools, you may need to encourage their use. This can look like taking advantage of them yourself, supporting employee requests, and enforcing benefits usage.

CARE SNAPSHOT 📷

OUR DEFINITION

Care is showing up in service of someone in a way that demonstrates that you value them enough to invest in their well-being, even when it isn't easy or convenient.

KEY TAKEAWAYS

- Caring *about* our people is not enough; we must care *for* them.
- We must get to know someone to care for them in a meaningful way.
- Care ≠ Nice
  - Care is rooted in service; it's about intentionally showing up even and especially when it's uncomfortable.
  - Niceness is rooted in appearance; it's about being polite and avoiding discomfort.
- Care is often most powerful when we show up for people during life's challenges.
- Caring leaders improve employee engagement, job performance, physical and mental health, well-being, and even the lifespan of their people.
- Teams where care thrives enjoy higher team morale, loyalty, and connection.

WHAT GETS IN THE WAY

- The stories we tell ourselves
- Time scarcity
- Hypercompetitive workplaces
- A quid pro quo mentality
- A "you go first" mentality
- Outdated ideas of strength

PRACTICE MAKES PROGRESS

- **Individual Practices**
  - Block out time for connection.
  - Get to know someone better.
  - Check your intentions.
- **Team-Wide Practices**
  - Create an expectation of connection.
  - Budget for care surprises.
  - Align behavior with systems.

CHAPTER 7

Embodiment #4: Gratitude

Wear gratitude like a cloak, and it will feed every corner of your life.
—**Rumi**

Gratitude is a form of mindfulness that focuses our attention on what we appreciate in ourselves, in our relationships, and in the world around us.

We share a hardwired human need to feel heard, seen, and valued, and gratitude is essential in creating spaces where that's the norm. While at first glance, "I'm grateful for the coffee you brought me this morning," may appear to be nothing more than a wordy "Thanks!" gratitude is far more than simple expressions of appreciation.

Gratitude combines mindset and action. It directs our attention and energy to notice more of what we appreciate about ourselves, our relationships, and the world around us. You can think of your gratitude practice as an activity that in the moment brings a smile, but also creates a collection of moments that you can always return to, to bring you joy. In the best of times, it's an act of cherishing moments. When life is most challenging, it's a silver-lining lens.

Everyone has experienced moments of feeling undervalued or unappreciated. Recently, many have shared concern that they don't matter or even described feeling invisible—especially at work.[1] Many of those tough feelings could have been largely prevented if people heard how others appreciate them or their work, and cultivating a team-wide culture of gratitude can help prevent them in the future. Gratitude also offers us the ability to cultivate increased well-being within ourselves. It has the power to rewire our brains, changing our relationship with ourselves and the world around us.

We all encounter challenges, especially at work. We all have ideas that get rejected. We all make mistakes. However, it's gratitude that empowers us to accept what is without staying focused on any associated suffering. When your project proposal is rejected, you can choose gratitude to focus on appreciation that you learned a new editing software that will be useful in the future. It isn't about denying it sucks to get rejected or pretending hard things aren't hard; it is about choosing to accept what is and noticing what we can appreciate in the present, which makes it easier to adapt moving forward. Now, more than ever before, it is important to be adaptable: to navigate uncertainty, to handle change, and to pivot intentionally.

Our brains often struggle handling change—and pivoting—as change comes with unknown and new risk. Despite their complex and beautiful capacities, at a base level, our brains were developed for a specific goal: to keep us alive. New environments, as well as unfamiliar information, are unmapped in our brains and therefore feel dangerous. This is why our brains are so good at finding reasons not to change. Our brains have evolved to pay close attention to, identify, and catalog potential threats. Studies have shown our brain responds more to negative images than to positive ones. And the more salient or emotionally charged an experience, the more likely our brain creates a lasting memory.[2] Psychologists Paul Rozin and Edward Royzman coined the term "negativity bias" in an influential 2001 publication to describe how negative events or experiences tend to have a greater impact on us.[3] This is one of the reasons why many of us can easily describe past negative experiences with incredible detail but struggle to recall a recent specific neutral or positive experience. Gratitude can help.

Studies show that gratitude has the power to rewire our brains to seek out and notice moments of goodness, joy, learning, and other positive experiences and perspectives.[4] Scholars have studied a wide array of the impacts of gratitude, and the results are incredibly promising. Beyond sociological and psychological research, doctors have even used functional MRIs to assist in mapping neurobiological responses related to gratitude.

Most often gratitude is external facing. We aim it toward nice weather or a kind colleague. But if you're anything like us we need to start closer to home. While this book is about leading, relating to, and teaming with others, your relationship with yourself is paramount—as highlighted in the relationship triangle. As we shared earlier, culturally, we value humility, especially in our leaders. Humility means recognizing our strengths and expertise as well as our weaknesses and areas for growth. Yet for many aspiring and successful leaders alike, we struggle with a nefarious barrier to humility.

If your idea of humility is a predominantly self-critical internal voice focused on what you want to fix about yourself (e.g., your behavior, appearance, work) and doesn't include self-appreciation or celebration for what you do well, we have some bad news for you: That's not humility; it's self-deprecation. Changing our internal voice and learning to embrace self-acceptance as a prerequisite for growth may be the most challenging shift of all—especially for ambitious, high-achieving perfectionists.

We don't know anyone who finishes their to-do list every single day or accomplishes everything they'd like to each week—we certainly never do. Since our brains' default is to focus on the risk to our belonging—which in the case of hustling to finish a to-do list translates to fixating on what we failed to get done—even if we accomplished 90 percent, we'll be disappointed. Frustration over not completing the last 10 percent without acknowledgement or celebration of the 90 percent we did do leads to constantly feeling behind or underwater.

JEAN

I am a recovering perfectionist, and while I like to think I'm more recovered than perfectionist, that hasn't been consistently true. Years ago, after starting my gratitude practice, I was filling a page of my gratitude journal daily. Then it hit me: I'd filled yet another page, and not even a single line expressed appreciation toward myself. As I flipped back through the pages and reflected, I realized I needed to include self-focused gratitude if I wanted to break the cycle of overlooking my progress and achievements. Since adjusting to include self-gratitude, this practice has helped me acknowledge my growth without costing my goals.

As much as leading is about those you lead, if you aren't willing to shift your internal voice, it is significantly more difficult to transform your authentic leadership. You cannot skip yourself if you want to become a transformative, human-focused leader.

So our challenge to you is to start right now. What's one thing you appreciate about yourself today? No need to write it or even share it. Just scan your day until this moment and pick one.

In case you need a spark to get going, we've got a few for you:

I read a book.
I set a boundary with so-and-so.
I went for a walk this morning even though I was tired.

And just as important:

I called in sick to rest because I'm fried.
I asked for help.
I said no to a social engagement.

We all are humans who deserve to give ourselves grace, celebrate wins (no matter how big or small), and appreciate what we do well, all of which can help with self-acceptance. As our brilliant friend

Dr. Laura Gallaher shares in her work, all the self-improvement in the world cannot compensate for (let alone resolve) low self-acceptance. Self-gratitude can shift our hardwired negativity bias and begin to strengthen new neural pathways key to self-acceptance, humility, and growth.

One 2017 study found that grateful people show stronger neural signatures of pure altruism in reward-system regions of the brain.[5] In simple terms, when we practice gratitude, we become less selfish and increasingly likely to give more without expectation of personal benefit. As author Melody Beattie puts it, "Gratitude unlocks the fullness of life. It turns what we have into enough, and more."

In addition to altruism, gratitude is connected to joy. When researchers at Stanford studied the connection between gratitude and joy, they found that "joy can increase gratitude and gratitude can increase joy, suggesting an 'intriguing upward spiral' between the two."[6] Essentially, in addition to strengthening our connections, rewiring our brains, and leading to more altruism, practicing gratitude can lead to a more joyful life.

Fleeting Happiness vs. Lasting Joy

Take a moment—think about how you would define happiness. Most of us know what *happy* feels like and can describe a happy moment in our life, yet when pushed to define it, we struggle.

Even in the research, among psychological experts and emotion researchers, there is no clear agreement on a definition of happiness. Happiness is often illustrated as an end state, an outcome to accomplish. *I'll be happy once I buy this big, fancy house* or *I'll be happy if my team wins the championship game.* Happiness is often described conditionally: If x happens, then I will be happy. Because it depends on external forces, happiness is fleeting. (New houses bring their own challenges and lose their luster; the excitement of a championship season wears off.) The external forces that make us happy are outside of our control. What happens if I can't afford the big, fancy house? And what if, during the championship game, we lose to a rival? The downsides are often hard-hitting and go beyond simply feeling unhappy.

Joy, on the other hand, is something we can consistently cultivate internally, regardless of external forces. Remember, gratitude is a form of mindfulness that focuses our attention on what we appreciate in ourselves, our relationships, and the world around us. So even when things don't go according to plan, gratitude helps us focus on what does evoke joy. You can't afford that fancy house now? You can be grateful you still have your current home in a neighborhood you love. Your team didn't win the championship? You can still be grateful they made it this far and played so well all season. You can be unhappy your team lost and still cultivate joy, which strengthens your resilience. The more resilient we are to external things not going our way, the more we diminish the weight of unhappiness.

Gratitude is a tool we can use to infuse more joy into our lives, our relationships—and our workplaces.

Cultivating a Culture of Gratitude

Gratitude is important in all our relationships, but it can have an especially profound ripple effect at work. A study from the *International Journal of Workplace Health Management* demonstrated that gratitude is a consistent predictor of:

- less exhaustion and less cynicism
- more proactive behaviors
- higher rating of the health and safety climate
- higher job satisfaction
- fewer absences due to illness[7]

There isn't anyone, any team, or any workplace that couldn't benefit from such improvements. As research continues to demonstrate their powerful impact on the health and well-being of teams as well as bottom lines, joy and gratitude are likely to become more commonly sought-after components of top-tier workplace cultures.

THE IMPACT OF A GRATEFUL LEADER

In modern workplaces, there is an expectation that junior employees should express gratitude toward senior members of the team for their time, attention, training, and so on. It's less common for senior team members to take the time to express gratitude to and acknowledge junior team members.

When senior leaders share authentic gratitude, it carries a lot of weight. We say *authentic* gratitude because people inherently notice and distrust inauthentic or perfunctory behavior. Perfunctory gratitude or saying a nice but insincere "thanks" can cause more damage than silence. When there's a sense that gestures are inauthentic, or that gratitude is unbalanced in a relationship, over time, it will drive disconnection. As leaders, we have the power to build a balanced team culture of gratitude.

Last year, our team met Jay, a CEO who shared his personal experience. During a meeting ten years prior, a VP of growth shared with Jay how hard Carolina, a young member of the team, had been working. She was, as he put it, "a glowing example of a team player." Jay pulled out a pile of sticky notes right then and there. "Carolina, I am grateful for all your extra effort and dedication to the organization," he wrote. "You are essential to everything we do here. Keep up the great work!" After the meeting wrapped and the office was nearly empty, Jay took a moment to walk the note over to Carolina's desk and stick it to her computer screen.

Five years later, Jay was floored to see that same sticky note framed and hanging on the wall in Carolina's new office. Carolina was now the VP of sales. It had taken him no more than a few moments to write that note, and although he hadn't considered it that big of a deal at the time, he now realized his simple expression of gratitude had made a bigger impact than he could've imagined.

As a leader, when you share gratitude and infuse it into your interpersonal relationships, it significantly influences the overall culture as well. It's in our nature to share what we are proud of, and it is quite an accomplishment to be noticed and appreciated by a top executive. Even a small moment of gratitude can ignite an upward spiral with a powerful ripple effect.

Think about the humans that surround you and dedicate themselves to setting you up for success: anyone from administrative assistants to VPs to frontline employees. It's important to make the time to articulate your gratitude, both publicly and in a one-on-one setting, for all they do and what they mean to you. Practicing this consistently over time can transform the culture of the entire organization.

> **A note**: Sure, receiving unexpected thoughtful gratitude feels great, but it takes time to develop a regular practice and attention

to remember to share it. As a leader with the goal to share more gratitude as a team, it can be helpful to regularly remind team members to get the conversation going. (For example, our team has a "high-fives & props" section in some meetings.) If you don't yet have a team gratitude practice, you can always request it in one-off settings too. Try something like, "I'm thinking about the last thirty days as fuel for my upcoming goals. Does any of my recent work stand out? I'd love to know what you see as my strengths." Waiting and hoping for your unspoken needs to be met often leads to disappointment and can ultimately build resentment. So break the stereotype that in good relationships people can read minds and get the ball rolling yourself!

Beyond "Thanks!"

The more we use words and phrases, the more they evolve into idioms or reflexive statements. *Thanks* is a perfect example. Expressing thanks is great, but it has become a reflex rather than an expression of true gratitude. Some of us say it a dozen or more times a day without even realizing it. It's akin to nodding and saying, "What's up?" or "How are you?" as you walk by with no intention of stopping to hear an actual answer. It's a simple, nice acknowledgment.

Compare that to when you actually take the time to sit down with a dear friend who is going through something difficult. Perhaps you put a hand on their shoulder or give them a caring look. In this case, when you ask, "What's up?" or "How are you?" you truly want an answer. This time, the words hold more weight. When you genuinely and intentionally seek to communicate and connect with someone, how you say something and the surrounding context make all the difference in the world, even when using the exact same words.

The same is true for gratitude. You may have said "thanks" or "appreciate it" to a fellow team member during quick exchanges throughout the week (or even your entire working relationship), but that's not the same as pausing and holding space to express how grateful you are for something they do, how they show up, or who they are. You may still use the words *thank you* or *appreciate it* rather than the word *grateful*, and that's okay. The particular words are not as important as taking the time, setting your intention, and sharing your gratitude.

Gratitude can sound like:

- It means so much to me that you took the time to help me with this hard situation.
- Thanks for your contribution to this project; I wouldn't have been able to meet the deadline or get it done as well without you.
- I appreciate your attention to detail. It really frees me up to get creative on the big picture.
- I'm thankful that you're always up to pitch in.

The above examples express an awareness and appreciation of others and their actions, which is key to a healthy interpersonal gratitude practice.

We're not saying you should give up on frequent expressions of *thanks* and *I appreciate it*. These gestures are still a piece of the puzzle for a collaborative, engaged, and warm workplace culture. In addition to the common and quick nods of recognition though, it is important to create the time and space for deeper conversations on gratitude if we want to encourage a culture of gratitude, a workplace with more joy, and better outcomes across the board.

Imagine if Jay had simply written "Thanks! —Jay" on his note to Carolina. Would that have felt nice? Yeah, but would it have ended up framed? Probably not.

What Gets in the Way

TAKING THINGS FOR GRANTED

Whether it's a service worker who consistently does his job well, a family member who never fails to offer a ride when needed, or the small conveniences of day-to-day living, when something becomes expected and dependable, we can easily take it for granted. We are all guilty of it. Yes, the barista is paid to make your latte, but does she have to do it with a smile and attention to detail? Sure, your mom loves to pick you up and cook you your favorite meal when you visit, but she may have to rearrange her day to do so. While safe, drinkable tap water is all you've ever known, that's a modern marvel millions still don't have.

TIME SCARCITY

In today's culture, we tend to move fast and fill up our calendars with more than we can handle. When we tell ourselves the story that we don't have time, we believe it. Without prioritization and making the time to do something, it will not happen, which reinforces the idea that there "just isn't enough time in the day." Feeling short on time is a common stressor, but this self-fulfilling narrative of constantly feeling behind only holds us back.

CONTEMPT

Feeling powerless, unheard, or overlooked is all too common at work. Unfortunately, over time and under bad management, it is easy to build up resentment and even contempt. When we reach a point where we feel contempt toward anything or anyone, we are in trouble. The Gottman Institute describes contempt as the most destructive negative behavior in relationships. "Contempt, simply put, says, 'I'm better than you. And you are lesser than me.'"[8] If we feel contempt toward a company or a person, the probability of finding the capacity for gratitude is low.[9]

Practice Makes Progress

INDIVIDUAL PRACTICES

Establishing a daily gratitude practice has tremendous benefits and the potential to transform how you show up in relationships. It can be as simple as acknowledging how much it brightens your day when you get a great parking spot or when the sun breaks through clouds. When we expand our daily practice to include gratitude for another human, the benefits grow exponentially. With that in mind, let's explore a few ways to practice gratitude.

Start Small

Create a gratitude journal. While it may be tempting to aim high and write fifteen moments, experiences, or people you're grateful for on day one, we recommend starting with three to five. Seek new experiences to write each day. Although it may be difficult on day three to come up with the twelfth "new" experience that week, it gets easier. As you seek more things to be grateful for, you expand the lens that notices details worthy of gratitude. If there is a particularly wonderful day and you feel inspired to write more, go ahead and do so. Give yourself space to expand when you're inspired, without the pressure of taking on too much too fast.

An end-of-day gratitude journal might look like this:

- I am grateful for my kid's thoughtful allergist for making today's appointment easy on us.
- I am grateful that I ended the day on inbox zero.
- I am grateful that Zoom didn't ask for any updates today.

Invite Others In

After you've made your list, share it! Pick one specific statement that expresses what you appreciate about someone you feel close to and share it with them.

- To the guy in the mail room ➤ *I am grateful for your timely and organized delivery.*
- To my assistant ➤ *I am grateful for your help with my calendar.*
- To the boss ➤ *I am grateful for the opportunity to shadow you on this.*

Inviting others into our gratitude practice allows us to see the positive impact it has on others firsthand. Beyond those you share gratitude with, another way to invite others in is by asking a trusted friend to check on your progress.

Focus on Impact

Focus on impact when expressing gratitude. Don't just say thanks; speak to why you're grateful. As we explained earlier, saying thanks is nice but often perfunctory. When you take the time to get explicit and expand on the specific impact that you are grateful for, it makes a world of difference.

Thank someone for what they did or said (or how they showed up) and then tell them about the positive impact (e.g., *"When you texted me five minutes before the huddle this week, it helped pull me out of my creative vortex; I would have missed the meeting again. Our boss was so mad at me last time; I am grateful that you get me and have my back!"*)

Let's break it down:

- To the assistant
    - » **Act:** I am grateful for your help with my calendar.
    - » **Impact:** I am grateful that, because of your attention to detail and ability to juggle priorities, I don't ever have to worry about missing meetings. Your help is such a relief.
- To the boss
    - » **Act:** I am grateful for the opportunity to shadow you on this.
    - » **Impact:** I am grateful for your continued mentoring on my public speaking skills. To be honest, I wouldn't be the professional I am today without your guidance. Thank you.

TEAM-WIDE PRACTICES

Build In Weekly Gratitude Conversations

One effective way to embed gratitude into your team's culture is by initiating weekly gratitude conversations. Set aside a few minutes at the end of each week for team members to share something they are grateful for—whether it's a colleague's support on a project, a recent achievement, or a small win that brought joy. Encourage everyone to contribute by providing an inviting, low barrier to entry. These conversations can be a great reminder of the good things happening around you, enhancing team morale and fostering a sense of camaraderie and appreciation.

Infuse Gratitude into Feedback

Most of our conversations around reviews and promotions are based on past performance and perceived improvement areas. While these are valuable insights we need, we also should be made aware of the positive impact we're having on those around us. Focus on sharing gratitude for what was done well (or is going well) in conjunction with what should be done better next time. If you have a way of surveying teammates for peer-to-peer feedback, include a prompt to share a bit of gratitude.

Create Spaces for Gratitude

Create a channel, thread, or board in a shared space. Whether a physical bulletin board or a virtual one in a platform like Slack or Teams, design it for people to share their gratitude. Virtual spaces allow for cool features like video notes, reaction emojis, and even the ability to create threads where others can build onto the posts they find. Automations can also remind teammates to add some appreciation, assign a random teammate to connect, share gratitude, and celebrate teammates, projects, and wins. Physical spaces are great for making it tangible—use them to highlight team creativity with photos, artwork, or handwritten notes.

Spaces that highlight specific acts of kindness, recognize hard work, or simply appreciate the presence and positivity of a teammate, over time, become a sort of monument of positive reinforcement. They boost morale and foster a sense of community. By regularly contributing to and reading a gratitude board, team members are reminded of the positive impact they have on one another. And since they have a place to put their own notes of gratitude, it encourages them to look for the good in those around them as well.

GRATITUDE SNAPSHOT 📷

OUR DEFINITION

Gratitude is a form of mindfulness that focuses our attention on what we appreciate in ourselves, in our relationships, and in the world around us.

KEY TAKEAWAYS

- Gratitude is a mindset and practice that shifts our focus toward appreciation and joy.
- Gratitude helps us build emotional resilience and adapt to challenges, due in large part to how it can counterbalance our negativity bias.
- Self-gratitude helps us balance self-criticism and avoid self-deprecation.
- While fleeting happiness depends on external outcomes, gratitude helps us cultivate lasting joy.
- Gratitude strengthens trust, reduces cynicism, and improves well-being.
- Leaders who model gratitude create a ripple effect that transforms team culture, strengthens relationships, and inspires gratitude in others.
- Intentional expressions of gratitude, especially when focused on the felt impact, are particularly meaningful.

WHAT GETS IN THE WAY

- Taking things for granted
- Time scarcity
- Contempt

PRACTICE MAKES PROGRESS

- **Individual Practices**
  - Start small.
  - Invite others in.
  - Focus on impact.

- **Team-Wide Practices**
  - Build in weekly gratitude conversations.
  - Infuse gratitude into feedback.
  - Create spaces for gratitude.

CHAPTER 8

Embodiment #5: Ownership

All we have to do to create the future is to change the nature of our conversations, to go from blame to ownership, and from bargaining to commitment, and from problem solving to possibility.
—Peter Block

Ownership integrates three elements: the external systems that set and hold us to standards, personal agency over our actions, and internal motivation.

The word *ownership* has many different definitions and interpretations—from a legal right to kinship, possession, independence, and so on. Depending on where you hear it and how it's used, its meaning varies wildly. At work, for example, there are a few main roles it plays. Taking ownership of a mistake means being accountable for it and accepting the consequences. Owning a role or project can mean having the autonomy to execute it as we see fit. Feeling a sense of ownership in a project or organization means that we feel a sense of responsibility for its success. No single use of ownership exists in a vacuum, nor does any single example above fully encompass ownership—especially in how it strengthens connections in our relationships and workplaces.

To illustrate the full picture of the kind of ownership we want to cultivate individually, interpersonally, and across our teams, we developed our own definition as a framework to facilitate better communication and cultivate robust ownership.

Another one for the formula lovers:

ACCOUNTABILITY + AUTONOMY + RESPONSIBILITY = OWNERSHIP

In terms of ownership, accountability, autonomy, and responsibility are interconnected. Even when we don't directly discuss all of them, they still influence how we set expectations, work to meet them, and review our part in achieving or failing to meet those expectations.

When we neglect to address all the elements of ownership, we block the transformational power of embodied ownership. Even worse is when we hold a narrow, one-sided view of ownership, for example accountability, while demanding ownership from someone who equates ownership with autonomy. It causes confusion, misalignment, and disconnection. Depending on the context and frequency of these kinds of misaligned conversations, it can also lead to interpersonal attacks and even high conflict, which further damages the relationship and obstructs ownership.

Just as ownership can mean different things to different people in different contexts (and those people may not even realize they're working from different understandings), there is also no universal agreement on what accountability, autonomy, and responsibility mean, either. For example, *Cambridge* includes "responsibility" but not "accountability" in its various definitions of ownership, while *Merriam-Webster* uses both interchangeably in a single definition of ownership—no wonder no one's aligned.[1] So to ensure we are all on the same page, we're going to break down what we mean to illustrate how each one of the elements of ownership points to a specific and intertwined piece of our internal world, external guardrails, and our personal agency.

Accountability

By accountability, we mean the systems—be it rules, laws, processes, technology, or other people—that hold us answerable to expressed standards. Typically, this is done by implementing consequences for not meeting those standards.

When someone breaks the law, they can be held accountable by the courts through fines or jail time. If an employee breaks company policy, they can be held accountable by formal warnings, demotions, and firings. And yes, even though accountability is externally applied, it is possible to hold yourself accountable. For example, if you want to stop swearing, you might implement a swear jar where you have to put in ten dollars each time you swear. By doing so, you are leveraging an external system that enacts clear consequences for a set standard.

At work, we are typically good at establishing codes of conduct, rules and regulations, and performance expectations for how people should act on the job and the consequences for when they aren't met. A boss is usually tasked with holding subordinates accountable to act in alignment with the company's standards and expectations by using tools like evaluations, promotions, and performance plans to enact consequences. However, not all consequences are created equally nor are all consequences connected to accountability. Unexpected consequences, or worse, punitive punishments, for not meeting unexpressed expectations, while common, hinder rather than help ownership.

Accountability requires that we know what is expected and the potential consequences. When we take the time to express a need and set a standard, and someone still fails to deliver, accountability does include consequences. In fact, the conversation, consequences, and next steps offer an opportunity to learn, grow, and strengthen the relationship. Even as you share the consequences, when there is true accountability (which includes owning your part), it increases their respect for your integrity. Conversely, unexpected punishments, such as yelling at someone for failing to meet an unexpressed need, shut down ownership, damage the relationship, and lead to increased fear of unpredictable outbursts.

We experience this at a personal level too. Whether the relationship is familial, friendly, or even collegial, we more often than not don't have performance improvement plans or bonuses to hold people accountable. Sometimes relational accountability simply means knowing that if someone breaks a promise —or if we're feeling uneasy about something they said or did—we can discuss it with them. Healthy relational accountability often starts (and even ends) with hard conversations about aligning expectations and agreeing on what we need moving forward. And if aligning via conversation doesn't lead to the change or impact we need, we can align on a new consequence moving forward.

For example, say your colleague agreed to finish building out a design template by Monday at 10:00 a.m. To add copy, you need the finished template, but when you open the template to get started at 10:30 on Monday morning, it isn't done. The first step in holding him accountable could start with talking to him about it: "Hey, Mark, I wanted to check in on the status of the template build. As you know, I need to add the copy by end of business today." If the conversation results in a plan to adjust timing so it works for everyone, then a conversation may be enough. On the other hand, what if Mark admits that he left early for dinner plans on Friday and that he's also a bit hungover this morning (and it's the third time he's broken a commitment to deliver work on time)? Holding him accountable might require alerting HR or the boss.

While accountability addresses unmet expectations, true ownership requires more than external consequences. This is where autonomy comes in: Empowering people to make decisions and shape outcomes fosters deeper investment in their work.

Autonomy

Autonomy is the freedom to determine if and how we solve problems and engage with our environment and the people around us. Our ability to make our own choices and feel a sense of personal control in our lives is a core human need. A meta-analysis published in 2011 examined well-being in sixty-three societies, and its authors Fischer and Boer found that autonomy is more important for national well-being than wealth—a sense of control is a universal predictor of lower anxiety levels.[2]

In addition to its societal influence, autonomy affects us individually as well. The amount of autonomy we feel over our work and in our relationships affects how we feel about each. Often, the level of autonomy that a boss gives us on a project is representative of how much they trust us. And in situations where trust is being built between a boss and subordinate, increasing autonomy provides an opportunity for us to increase trust in ourselves and each other. Conversely, restricting autonomy can inhibit ownership and can undermine feeling trusted.

How many times have we heard a boss or manager extoll the value of employees feeling a sense of ownership in their work, only to micromanage every decision those employees make on the job? Such an environment decreases personal agency and makes it likely that employees feel their boss doesn't trust them to do the work they were hired to do.

When we can make choices that affect the way we work and the outcomes of that work—when we have autonomy—we often feel more like owners. Even if it's not nefarious, when we lack autonomy and are stripped of our power and control, we're one step closer to disengagement.

MATT

Over the years, I've been asked to emcee and/or conduct ceremonies for friends and family. From retirement parties to weddings and funerals, one of the biggest factors affecting how I feel about leading an event is how much autonomy I'm given.

On the one hand, I've had people say, "Here are the must-haves.

Here's some additional context. With that in mind, we trust you to make it great!" In those scenarios, I'm at my best. I can speak authentically. I can respond and roll with surprises more naturally. And when I do that, I better connect with the other people there, resulting in a much better experience for everyone involved.

On the other hand, I've had some people say, "I know you're comfortable speaking in front of audiences, so we trust you not to freeze up. Here's the agenda and a script of exactly what to say, when to say it, and how to handle some expected scenarios. Thanks!" And while I can appreciate someone wanting their event to go exactly how they imagined it, when I'm given a script, I come off robotic. I worry about not messing up rather than delivering something powerful and special. My ability to show up authentically disappears, and as a result, the experience I can create for people is diminished. And the worst part is I'm not as invested in how well it goes.

Just as Matt didn't feel those scripted speeches were his, without autonomy our work doesn't *feel* like it's ours. When we experience micromanagement, it's hard to feel proud of great work or guilty for bad work—because we didn't have enough personal agency to influence the work. And in these types of situations, it's easier for us to dismiss negative feedback or to deflect blame, since the work genuinely feels less like it's our own.

While we often think about autonomy in more creative work endeavors—like copywriting, visual design, or vendor and product selection—autonomy can play an important role in many other jobs that are traditionally standardized as well. As an example, think about a convenience store clerk. Often when stepping into such a role, there are strict guidelines around things like how and when to restock shelves, take breaks, and clean things up. And while there is certainly a need to be strict with things like managing the cash drawer or checking IDs on certain purchases, there are other ways that the clerk can be empowered through autonomy.

Rather than giving a specific list of tasks and times to do each (e.g., mop the bathroom at 5:05, stock the cooler at 5:45, refill coffee at 6:15, and so on) you can train them around clear priorities. You can offer a sheet with guidance that includes qualitative goals to guide their behavior such as objectives and some tips for what you've seen work well in the store before. It could be a sheet that reminds them that you want customers to have a positive experience, find their desired drinks chilled in the right spot, have a clean and orderly environment, and leave with smiles on their faces.

> *Our main goal is to make customers feel welcomed, easily find what they want, and leave with smiles on their faces. That could mean saying hello when a customer walks in, striking up a light conversation while at the register, or a simple smile. Please stock the coolers when you notice them getting low and have a free moment.*
>
> *Do periodic checks in the bathrooms to make sure supplies are at good levels and to do light cleaning. Don't forget to check the coffee around 4 p.m. to be ready for the evening rush! Lastly, if you're on the closing shift, there is a checklist of things to get done before locking up. That checklist is attached.*

Autonomy is not binary; it's a dimmer switch that needs careful adjustment for success. Many factors impact the ideal amount of autonomy in a given role. Here are just a few examples:

- Scope and impact of a role or project
- Legal ramifications of getting something wrong
- Role holder's desired amount of autonomy
- Role holder's relationship with the manager
- Current organizational objectives
- Track record within a team, organization, or industry

We list these examples to call out that autonomy can, and often needs to, be demonstrated differently based on the circumstances. There is no such thing as one-size-fits-all autonomy. The most important thing to remember is to integrate autonomy that promotes adequate freedom for the individual, given their specific context.

Responsibility

Responsibility is an internal drive that motivates us to show up in certain ways, treat people appropriately, and create certain outcomes. It can be described as a feeling of duty or onus. It inspires us to take action, even when there may be no explicit expectation for us to do so. It's the thing that gets us out of bed even when we are tired. Unlike accountability, which can be applied externally even under protest, and autonomy, which can be granted or infringed upon by others, your sense of responsibility is exclusively generated within you—and no one else can force you to feel it.

This is why so many leaders struggle to cultivate responsibility within their people. Whether someone feels it or not is entirely up to that person. For example, if I don't feel internally motivated to take on a task or mentor an intern, my boss can't say or do anything to force me to feel differently. But, since my boss can change the incentive or consequence to get a desired outcome, she can influence my behavior. Unlike internal motivators, behavior is clearly visible and easy to measure, which can create blind spots for managers who assume their time-tested tactics that drive behavior change are motivating their people, even when they may be doing the opposite. Without getting to know what drives your people, you'll stay unaware of how or when their responsibility levels are high or low.

We often hear business owners looking for ways to get their team members to act like owners, which typically translates to, "We want you to be as excited and passionate about the business's success as we are!" or "We want you to go above and beyond—to treat this company like your baby as much as I do." The simple truth is, it's not "their baby" and it's uncommon for employees to feel the same way about the business as its founder. While it's reasonable to aim for increased engagement and even passion from your people, there is no one-size-fits-all copy-and-paste option that works.

The motivators that drive our responsibility are diverse, often interconnected, and can change over time. So what inspires one person's sense of responsibility in a given scenario is often different from, and potentially even diametrically opposed to, what inspires responsibility for another person in that same scenario. Some of us are driven by moments of joy, fun, and laughter, while others might be driven by a sense of purpose and a desire to make an impact. Others still are driven by things like achievement, status, or economic goals. Even within a group of ambitious salespeople who respond well to competition, they each might be driven by different motivators, such as winning bragging rights, earning more money, or gamifying an otherwise monotonous task.

As leaders, it is important to know the contributing factors that foster a sense of responsibility for each of our team members. While you may not be able to make someone feel responsible, getting to know someone on a deeper level—understanding their values and their motivations—allows you to better assign work and coach them in a way that connects to their internal drivers and motivations. And if we can better match people with work, communicate in a way that drives passion and motivation, and help them get unstuck when levels of responsibility might be getting low, we maximize our odds of increasing responsibility across the entire team.

OWNERSHIP IN 3D

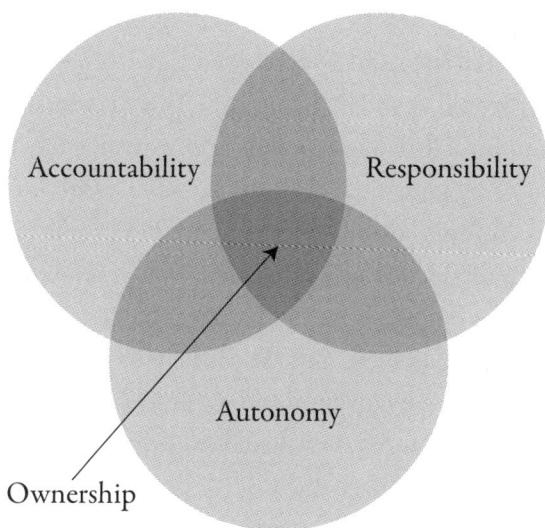

Accountability, autonomy, and responsibility each have intrinsic value individually. Increased awareness and balance of these three elements together have hugely positive effects on our relationships and throughout our workplaces. While having all three isn't always an option for us in every instance, when we can cultivate all three, it shifts how we show up and develops the kind of ownership that transforms our relationships and workplaces.

When each person feels responsible for the relationship, has the autonomy to make choices about how they show up, and holds themselves and one another accountable, it's a powerful shift toward embodied ownership.

Cultivating a Culture of Ownership

Picture this: You come to work on Monday morning to an office filled with people who trust one another. When managers assign work, they are confident they have trained their employees well enough to make the right choice, even if it's different from the choice they would've made themselves. There is transparent and clear communication about needs and expectations from the onset to ensure alignment and continued touchpoints on progress. Employees don't play the blame game, and they expect to hold one another accountable for issues that arise. When someone makes a mistake or steps out of bounds with their behavior, they raise their hand, call themselves on it, and ask for help to resolve it. Leaders and employees alike are invested and motivated in doing their best work and contributing to shared goals together.

Now *that's* a workplace that doesn't suck.

While the workplace above may be hard to imagine if our past work experiences have been significantly different, these places do exist, and you can help build one, too. When we each personally embrace ownership, develop bidirectional ownership in our one-on-one relationships, and infuse ownership into group and team settings, we create a culture of multidirectional ownership. This means that managers aren't the only ones that can hold people accountable.

Team members need to be able to hold managers accountable as well. We are all in it together, working side by side to accomplish shared goals.

The same is true for autonomy. If only managers have the freedom to do their work as they see fit while everyone else is prohibited from making meaningful choices in their work, ownership breaks down. Managers must create an environment where levels of autonomy exist in every role. Finally, we cannot expect employees to feel motivated, inspired, and responsible for the business if the manager doesn't feel those things as well. And if any of us are struggling to connect with our sense of responsibility, we can collaboratively work on finding a way to reignite the spark.

While internal reflection is a great start, there is no avoiding talking about each element of ownership with each other to cultivate an embodied ownership culture. This framework can provide the scaffolding to help start the conversation. By having open, honest, and consistent communication—from setting expectations, to understanding who's driven and has bandwidth, to extending trust and giving space to work—we ensure alignment. This way, we each know what is expected of us, what we are and aren't allowed to do in pursuit of those expectations, and what consequences exist if we don't meet the expectations.

Ownership goes beyond a workplace concept. It's a mindset that transforms how we approach challenges, relationships, and growth. Whether in business or in life, embracing ownership gives us the power to shape our circumstances, build trust, and lead with integrity. When we blend accountability, autonomy, and responsibility, we don't just improve our teams; we create environments where we can count on one another.

What Gets in the Way

FEAR OF LOSS

Whether it's our job or a personal relationship, it's natural to fear loss. When we depend on someone for our livelihood, social connection, or well-being, it may be difficult to believe we can hold them accountable. When the perceived risk of loss outweighs the potential reward, this creates a barrier to the practice of ownership.

HYPOCRISY

Hypocrisy undermines a culture of ownership. Ownership cannot thrive in an environment where it's okay when the boss does it but not okay when other people do it. Any time a boss demands accountability and responsibility from others but not themselves, or demands autonomy for themselves while micromanaging others, you slam the door on ownership.

MICROMANAGEMENT

Most of us have felt micromanaged at some point in our lives. Perhaps it was from a boss who controlled every single detail of an assigned project (down to the fonts used in emails). Maybe it was during a date night with your partner when you decided to cook a dish together, and they just couldn't stop themselves from looking over your shoulder to make sure you prepared everything the exact way they would. When we do not trust others to make independent decisions, we curtail their autonomy and stifle their sense of ownership.

LACK OF CLARITY

Clarity is kindness and holds the key to empowerment. Without clarity from management or stakeholders, no employee is set up for success. We often hear leaders say, "I expect people to be self-starters," or "I like to let them learn through doing," or even "They should know; it's obvious." Let us be crystal clear: Expecting people to read minds and/or have the exact specs in their heads of what your unspoken needs and preferences are is unreasonable. Without clarity on the limits, must-haves, and context, there is no true autonomy or possibility of ownership. It doesn't have to be long and complicated, but it must be clear.

Practice Makes Progress

INDIVIDUAL PRACTICES

Try the 3Q (Three-Question) Method

When given a new project, task, or role, evaluate your levels of ownership with a quick three-question review.

1. **Are we clear on who is accountable for what and what consequences there are for falling short?** Has it been formally stated? If not, it's time to make that clear.
2. **Are we aligned on how much autonomy I have in the project/task?** Has it been formally stated? If not, it's time to make that clear.
3. **How motivated do I feel about this task/project/role?** Why is it at that level, and if it needs to change, how can I do that?

Scan for Imbalance

Whether you've already experienced burnout or not, to prevent it, you can leverage ownership to identify what drains you versus what energizes you. Is too much of your day spent on tasks you feel little to no excitement about?

If you lack motivation for everything and are experiencing acute burnout, it's time for a break. However, if you are one of the millions who enjoy certain aspects of your job and day but feel stuck doing too much of what drains you—or feel overwhelming stress at work—knowing whether you feel excessive or insufficient responsibility will give you a clearer idea of where to start.

Is burnout common with your colleagues as well? Are there clear inefficiencies in processes, multiple unfinished to-dos (blocked by one person, a team, or a lack of resources), or simply too many diverging priorities? Is there a lack of accountability from upper management?

Using this framework to highlight where there is an imbalance in accountability, autonomy, and responsibility and adjust accordingly sets us up to stop burnout and break the cycle.

Normalize "No"

People need to be able to say no. If you are the person in a position of authority on the team, your responses to these moments will either reinforce or undermine ownership. You have to celebrate the nos and clearly show how they are essential to create the space to do the yeses well! Create the space for these dialogues by taking five minutes to check in on three key aspects: the practical piece (necessary resources for getting started), the human aspect of bandwidth (energy and time), and the project/task owner's levels of accountability, autonomy, and responsibility. Going through this helps us realize when we are and aren't set up for success, making the *no* easier to deliver and understand.

TEAM-WIDE PRACTICES

Draft Clear Guidelines

To make sure the team is on the same page, it's crucial to set, share, and reinforce team-wide norms and expectations. It's okay to consider things on a case-by-case basis and make exceptions, but if there are no exceptions, be transparent about who owns what, when, and why. Especially in busy environments, a lack of clear norms and guidelines diminishes ownership. People often make assumptions instead of interrupting to clarify once they begin; or they just wait when they don't see a clear path forward, leading to delays and misalignment. This is why it's a good idea to designate, verbally or graphically, the person people should go to for different needs or obstacles. For example, your CSMs should go to Jeff in IT for a technical bug or blocker, or the sales team should direct all copy doubts to Margie in marketing. This fits nicely into a clear org chart and helps alleviate stress caused by uncertainty. Clear, transparent guidelines and guardrails empower ownership for individuals and the greater team.

Create a Knowledge Base

For recurring tasks and projects that require back-and-forth, multiple edits, and feedback sessions, invest effort upfront to ensure your team gets the job done correctly and on time. As leaders, the better we get at building and communicating the team's sandbox—the boundaries, available tools, rules, and norms—ahead of time on any given project, the higher the likelihood of success.

One great way to get started is to create a knowledge base—an accessible electronic source of truth—that includes clear documentation with both quantitative and qualitative information, so an assignee knows what it takes to do their task well. Be clear about needs, detail any processes, include previous learnings, and make it easy to update when new information comes up. Have an owner of each relevant part, so if they have clarifying questions, they go to the right person. Encourage iteration and improvement to any project or task in the knowledge base. Invite all collaborators to share feedback. For any project, setting the team up for success includes providing assignees with clarity on their accountability, confidence in where their autonomy begins and ends, and the opportunity to cultivate their internal responsibility.

Shift from Retros and Redos to Proactive Ownership

Meetings such as retrospectives or after-action reviews can be powerful tools for uncovering new learnings, evaluating progress, and iterating our tactics moving forward. For such reviews to be most valuable, they need to reflect previously discussed preferences, needs, and expectations. Rather than exclusively waiting to evaluate how things went until after they're done, set your team up for ownership success from the start. As a leader who wants to cultivate ownership in your teams, seek to understand a team member's preferred level of autonomy, what drives their sense of responsibility, and how to foster bidirectional accountability with them before assigning out work.

Be proactive, invest time in building relationships, and intentionally set your team on a path to ownership. Start now. And moving forward, leverage what you know about ownership to inform hiring, onboarding, and continued learning and development.

Explore what they need to feel empowered. Talk about what inspires and motivates them. The insights that come from creating a trusting relationship enable new ways to connect the work in front of us to the motivations within us. When we know someone's desired level of autonomy and what (if any) resources they may need, we can adjust accordingly. And as always, ensure that accountability conversations are tied to previously discussed standards, stated project expectations or team norms, and the corresponding consequences for not meeting them. Remember, unexpected punishments masquerading as accountability severely damage team morale and impinge individual and team ownership.

OWNERSHIP SNAPSHOT 📷

OUR DEFINITION

Ownership integrates three elements: the external systems that set and hold us to standards, personal agency over our actions, and internal motivation.

Accountability + Autonomy + Responsibility = Ownership

KEY TAKEAWAYS

- Ownership thrives when accountability, autonomy, and responsibility are aligned and actively practiced together.
- Misalignment in how people define or apply ownership leads to confusion, conflict, and even breakdowns in trust.
- **Accountability**: the systems that hold us answerable to clearly expressed standards, often by implementing consequences for not meeting those standards.
- **Autonomy**: the freedom to determine if and how we solve problems and engage with our environment and the people around us (i.e., personal agency).
- **Responsibility**: an internal drive that motivates us to show up in certain ways, treat people appropriately, and create certain outcomes (i.e., a feeling of duty or onus).
- Cultivating a culture of ownership requires that ownership flows in all directions—not just top-down.
- Embodied ownership transforms workplaces into environments of trust, dependability, and alignment.

WHAT GETS IN THE WAY

- Fear of loss
- Hypocrisy
- Micromanagement
- Lack of clarity

PRACTICE MAKES PROGRESS

- **Individual Practices**
  - Use the 3Q method.
  - Scan for imbalance.
  - Normalize "No."

- **Team-Wide Practices**
  - Draft clear guidelines.
  - Create a knowledge base.
  - Shift from reactive to proactive ownership.

CHAPTER 9

Where We Go from Here

Consistency is the secret sauce—taking small sometimes messy steps paves the way for bigger achievements in the long run.
—Felecia Etienne

While we have given you a lot of information to consider, the good news is you are already well on your way. There is a lot to learn, unlearn, try, mess up, repair, iterate, build upon, and so on, which at times may feel overwhelming. Transformation doesn't happen in giant steps but in micromoments and subtle shifts. No matter where you're starting from on your journey to embody curiosity, authenticity, care, gratitude, and ownership, you are closer than you may think.

AWARENESS ➤ PRACTICE ➤ HABIT ➤ EMBODIMENT

Expanding Awareness

It's typical to have different levels of awareness, practice, and habits with each embodiment. A great place to start is taking inventory of where you currently feel strong and where you know you have more work to do. Our friend Rich Diviney offers a great visual for this in his book *The Attributes*. He describes personal attributes as a set of dimmer switches on a wall. All of them have the same high and low settings. Naturally, some of these are higher for you: These would be your innate attributes. Other switches start at a lower level: These attributes will take more work, effort, and intention to improve.

The same is true for each of our embodiments. It's normal and human to have different innate strengths and areas for improvement. For instance, even after writing this book, we both (Matt and Jean) are still at different stages on the path for each of the five embodiments. We are works in progress. We learn more daily about how to be better leaders and better versions of ourselves as we actively practice and help each other with the parts we find most challenging. When we fall short, we remind ourselves *progress > perfection* and keep going.

As you reflect on your current relationship with each embodiment, consider the following questions:

- Do any of them already feel natural to you?
- Where do you find yourself struggling most?
- Are some of these easier for you at work versus at home or vice versa?
- What patterns do you notice in your leadership style?
  - » Which do you want to let go or change?
  - » Which would you like to build on or strengthen?
- How do others experience your leadership?

You'll notice that in that list of questions, there is one that you can't answer by yourself: *How do others experience your leadership?* Working with others in this process helps fill in a more complete picture of ourselves. We all have blind spots. While honest self-reflection can provide us a great foundation to build from, if we want to be better leaders of people, we'd better find out if there is a gap in our intention and the impact we have on our people. By learning about how they feel about our leadership and any areas they think we can improve, they help us see from new perspectives.

Once you have *awareness* of where your dimmer switch sits for each of the five embodiments, or any personal principle you aim to embody, you can make intentional choices about what to try next. Some good news is that the simple act of learning about and pursuing the five embodiments in and of itself will improve your relationships and leadership. Your willingness to explore these concepts and answer some potentially uncomfortable questions about yourself already sets you apart from the droves of bad bosses out there who refuse to take an honest inventory of themselves. Just imagine how much further ahead you'll get by continuing on the path to embodying curiosity, authenticity, care, gratitude, and ownership!

No matter what you discover about your current dimmer settings, keep in mind that even small steps forward have profound impacts on our relationships and our teams. Don't wait for the "right" time or think that you're starting too small for it to matter.

Exploring Practices

The practice phase is where we will spend most of our time as we work toward building habits and ultimately embodying these principles. This is because we'll be testing out what does and doesn't work for us. While some embodiments have a clear set of practices we can follow to get started, others require trial and error to find the practices that best fit us. For example, most gratitude practices start with "I am grateful (for/to) . . ." While the rest is up to you, the foundation of how and where to start is clear.

Practice can be difficult, not just because it's taking theory and putting into action, but also because there isn't a one-size-fits-all template available for every practice as there is with gratitude. While we've included a variety of practice ideas in each embodiment chapter, some may work great for you, and others may not. Try ours, try others, and ask trusted colleagues or mentors for ideas. By experimenting with different approaches and testing what does and doesn't resonate, you learn, expand your comfort zone, and find the practices that have the power to become life-changing habits.

Some practices can be planned, and others are in-the-moment situational responses. For example, I can set up recurring ownership conversations with my team to check in and ensure alignment on ongoing projects (planned) but cannot predict suddenly hearing the CTO assign a high-priority task to our team during an all-hands call that will not fit into our upcoming sprint (situational response). We cannot plan for every moment, and unscheduled curveballs are often inevitable at work. However, a well-rounded practice requires preparation. Preparing for how you might respond to scenarios like this before they happen helps you stay grounded and confident when handling these challenges.

In order to prepare for the unplanned or unexpected, set aside time to think through scenarios you have faced that challenged your team's culture of ownership and how you can navigate misaligned or excessive requests. You may already have some ideas for potential responses, such as "We'll check out capacity and commitments and get back to you by EOD tomorrow," or "What task(s)/project(s) would you like us to deprioritize to make space for this in the current sprint?" Sometimes a chaotic or overbooked call isn't the right place to have the conversation. Often a direct conversation with the involved parties afterward is best. This also provides the opportunity for you to build an agenda and prepare for that call.

As with any practice, whether it's something you can build into your schedule or a real-time response that you know will help you show up better in an unplanned interaction, the key is finding something that works for you. Practices are meant to be tried and tested; some will stick, others won't. Let go of what doesn't work, and keep moving forward toward strong habits with the ones that do.

Building Habits

Repetitively showing up (in a similar way and interval) helps transform practices into habits. Many fitness influencers insist on this type of repetition: *Rain or shine, good mood or bad, put on your sneakers for that 7:00 a.m. run—otherwise, you won't reach your goals.* But what happens when your alarm clock doesn't go off, your kid is up sick all night and has to stay home from school, or the morning roads are solid ice?

If we can be clear on our goals and stay flexible in how we get there, we'll be more likely to achieve the results we desire. After all, is the goal the early morning run itself? Or is it to improve cardiovascular health? Or to get outside, move, and spend time alone in the fresh air before desk work? In any case, we can get creative and find other ways to stay consistent in the pursuit of our goal—even if we've missed our run.

The transition from practice to habit occurs gradually, often so subtly that you might not notice it happening. The tipping point between practice and habit is when you no longer have to consciously decide to inject that practice into your day; you simply do it, instinctually. Even when you get bumped off course, the question is how you will adapt to maintain your habit rather than if you will do it.

You'll start adapting to different situations automatically, finding creative ways to maintain habits even when circumstances change. For example, when you're on vacation and forget to bring your gratitude journal along, the question is no longer whether you'll do it but rather how you will adapt (e.g., typing a note on your phone instead of writing it in your journal). In fact, moving through your day without doing some form of a gratitude practice might feel weird or incomplete. A good indicator of reaching the habit phase is that you feel odd or uncomfortable without it.

According to research, folks who have the most long-term success in maintaining good habits are the ones who have a plan but expect to adjust occasionally and stay flexible. It is the same with the embodiments. Our practices will shift and evolve depending on the people we are connecting with, the context we're operating in, and what is going on in our world. The important thing is not that it always looks the same but that you continue to work on living these embodiments consistently.

Reaching Embodiment

True embodiment of a principle represents a deeper level of integration where it becomes not just something you do, but part of who you are. When you reach this phase, these principles manifest naturally across every facet of your life.

For example, when we embody curiosity, it evolves from something that we *do* to being a core part of who we *are*. Beyond interjecting more questions into meetings and habitually exploring ways to better understand your friends, you begin to ooze inquisitiveness, from the way you approach conversations and decisions to the ever-evolving way you see the world and make those around you feel interesting and heard. Even beyond the walls of work, everything is an opportunity to learn something new, and you default to openness rather than judgment.

Embodiment is how we show up; it is a core part of us and radiates out of us. It is clear in what we say, the choices we make, the way we think, and how we spend our time. Everything from your decision-making process to handling a major team conflict inherently incorporates that principle.

The way you handle challenges becomes clear evidence of your embodied principles. When faced with setbacks, you don't need to consciously remember to stay curious or show gratitude—these responses become your new default. Your team interactions become consistently aligned with these principles, creating a reliable and trustworthy leadership presence that others can count on.

A great sign you're in the embodiment phase is that others describe you with adjectives of principles you embody. They see you as the personification of the principle and can attest to the observable impact of that principle in your life and on those around you. This isn't to say that you can't embody principles without the approval of others—you absolutely can. Approval and impact are different: Impact is about interpersonal relationships, while approval is about judgment of personal opinions. If you believe you embody care, but those around you don't feel cared for, the lack of impact is a sign something is amiss. However, if you believe you embody adventure, someone else's judgment of your version of adventure is irrelevant. Embodiment has tangible impact: When we truly embody our values, it will be noticed and felt by those closest to us.

Consistency

While a single interaction can inspire and spark an initial connection, individual moments don't build long-term change. Just like habits, lasting relationships take time to develop, and while habit-building lessons support achieving your relational goals, transformation, especially of ourselves and our relationships, requires a deeper understanding of consistency's additional dimensions.

Think about the most consistent person in your life. What makes them consistent?

As we thought about our answer to this question while writing this book, it was clear we weren't describing the person's routines.

JEAN

I spent a lifetime dancing, skiing, figure skating, playing sports, and practicing yoga all while misunderstanding balance—until a single moment shifted my perspective forever. At that point in my life, I was well into a regular yoga practice. I had found a studio, a community, and teachers I adored. I regularly practiced eight ninety-minute yoga classes per week.

Yoga teachers often tell their students to find ease, especially in challenging poses, which I didn't understand. I thought if I tried harder, practiced more—if I just became strong enough—I'd find the illusive ease they mentioned. When I couldn't master a challenging pose, I steadfastly practiced it. When I got it, people commented that I made it look easy.

Inside, however, my balance felt precarious. Between lifting away from the ground and simultaneously contracting inward for counterbalance, I exerted a lot of effort. I squeezed and pushed through every tiny corner of each finger, contorting and clenching different muscle groups to find perfect stillness, which was, in my mind, the gold standard of balance. Because of what I now know is a misguided and rigid definition of balance, I rarely found it, and balancing was unfamiliar to me. So when I found it, if only momentarily, it was amazing and fleeting. Often, I'd fall out of it quickly or let go when I felt I was about to fall.

Then one day, I had my contorted body carefully balanced in the air when my beloved teacher Sarah began to discuss balance. She told us that balance is not stillness, that true balance in fact requires space to sway. She described how lasting balance comes from having a strong center and trusting yourself to move within a safe-not-to-fall range.

In that moment, I was confronted with what I had thought balance was and just how misguided my definition was. I realized I was afraid of the very movement that would have helped me balance. I had been misinterpreting the small shifts in my body as indicators of a lack of balance and a pending fall. I was scared to fall, to fail, to look ridiculous. My idea of balance and fear of falling led me to fight against myself by trying to control and restrict my body and even my breath.

At that very moment, I realized I wasn't breathing. I hadn't inhaled. So I took a slow, deep inhale and felt my rib cage expand. As I filled my lungs with air, *I released tension and finally felt a lightness and found ease in my arm balance.*

That day, Sarah offered me a mirror to something I hadn't been able to see in myself and planted a seed that continues to grow and influence how I show up on and off the mat. That moment was a profound lesson that I still return to and is foundational to how I see consistency.

Just as balance is not forced stillness, consistency is not merely simple repetition.

True consistency is a living, breathing representation of our deeply rooted values. It is how we show integrity and cocreate psychological safety in our relationships and teams. Even as leaders, consistency does not require perfection; however, it does demand our best efforts to show up for the people around us. When we give this effort day in and day out—even when we miss the mark—we build trust, deepen connection, and show people that we are committed to being a steady, dependable presence for them.

Think back to the most consistent person you know. Was it their habits alone that earned them this position in your mind or something else?

For us, it isn't as much about a specific, repeatable behavior as it is about the alignment between who we know them to be and how they show up, act, and engage with the world. They are there for us, through ups and downs, even when it's inconvenient. They are good at regulating their emotions, so they don't blow up or overreact when faced with challenging obstacles or difficult people. They are the opposite of hypocritical; even when it may cost them something, they maintain integrity with their core values.

Consistency doesn't require that you become an inflexible, repetitive robot that makes no mistakes or never deviates from a behavior. In fact, it's impossible to sustain consistency that way. As Jean learned when dropping out of her arm balance when she was afraid to fall, when you force it, fake it, or move from fear, you don't just make it harder on yourself; you create the very barrier that will hold you back from embodiment. Sustainable consistency thrives when you trust yourself to sway within a safe-not-to-fall range around your core principles. Only when you have room to breathe and find ease can you stay on your desired track. Be steadfast in your core principle or goal—and flexible in how you meet it.

If you want to build sustainable relationships, the ones that don't just survive the test of time but actually *strengthen* through navigating challenges on their journey, balance and consistency are essential. Just as a strong bridge doesn't crumble under mild storms, strong relationships built with consistent character weather the moments when we fall short. These relationships allow mistakes to be seen exactly as they are—exceptions to a well-established rule.

In relation to the five embodiments, consistency shifts your default settings for how you show up and engage toward more curiosity, authenticity, care, gratitude, and ownership. It means that in good times or bad, you don't just transform yourself; you create opportunities for others to also thrive. The way you show up—at work, at home, in every interaction—has a ripple effect beyond what you can see. It's not about perfection. It's about showing up as the best version of yourself each and every day and embracing the opportunity to move toward the leader you aspire to be.

CHAPTER 10

Make the Relation*shift*

The desire to reach for the stars is ambitious.
The desire to reach hearts is wise.
—**Maya Angelou**

Strong relationships are long-term investments. Human-focused leadership is an ongoing commitment. Creating workplaces that don't suck won't happen overnight. And yet, at a time when these efforts are more critical than ever, they can also feel more daunting than ever. Globally we are experiencing mental health crises and a leadership deficit, alongside the declared loneliness epidemic in the United States. The weight of these challenges makes it easy to deprioritize relationship building, leadership development, and workplace transformation—especially when so much already feels uncertain and exhausting. Honestly, continued findings from leading institutes including Gallup, WHO, and the NIH—spanning industries, worker demographics, and both private and public sectors—have us quoting the Offspring: "The kids aren't alright."

All of this can overwhelm even the most optimistic of us, making it tempting to throw up our hands and say, "That's just how it is," while operating from the stance that accepting the current reality is the only rational thing to do, that it isn't worth it to swim upstream. Frankly, that is the stance most people take. It's a large part of why we are in a leadership deficit.

As human-focused leaders, we don't simply have the power to influence the way it is; we have a responsibility to be part of the solution. It all starts by showing up for the people around us. We can shift our mindset and choose to be the change we wish to see in the world. How we do that can be life changing. According to research, bosses have a greater impact on our well-being than even our doctors and therapists and as much as our spouses.[1] So, as leaders, even when it might not feel like we are changing the entire world, when we infuse our relationships with curiosity, authenticity, care, gratitude, and ownership, we do change the world for each and every one of our people.

Whether you're trying to build an industry titan that tops the Fortune 100 for years to come, looking for more innovative ways to design and deliver digital projects, or trying to level up your leadership through turbulent times, relationships are foundational. The Five Embodiments are the key to cultivating strong, sustainable relationships that become the pillars of your team and help bring your vision to life.

Catalyzing any change is hard. The gamble feels more reasonable when you can visualize the gains; the burden is lighter when it's collectively shared; and vulnerability is less frightening when we know that we're surrounded by people who have our backs. As more individual team members show up curious, authentic, caring, grateful, and in ownership, the impact will spread. It just needs a spark to start it all.

As modern, human- focused leaders, it's up to us to create that spark: to set the tone, loudly and unapologetically modeling a new approach to leading and living. Reaching the tipping point is in your grasp. It just takes that first ally to make the process easier and more impactful. We can attest—we speak from experience.

Our Relation*shift*

Before teaming up to write this book, we spent years working together, discovering we had a lot in common and developing a strong friendship. We both were the youngest in our families, grew up playing competitive sports, *might* have been teachers' pets, and traveled extensively. As ambitious overachievers, we unsurprisingly also have strong opinions.

Between these commonalities and our aligned vision for how the world of work needed to evolve, we decided that embarking on the process of writing a book together seemed like a no-brainer. After all, we'd spent years working together, building programs and experiences to help organizations develop more human-focused leaders. So we were extremely (perhaps even *naively*) optimistic about how easy writing a book together would be.

Two people trying to build an inspiring manuscript that blends both authors' voices, drives real impact, and feels like a pride-worthy representation of each person involved is already a difficult task. But that same ambition and strong will that brought us together also fueled debate and frustration—over which concepts were most important to the book, what was fast enough versus too rushed, and even whose color preferences on the cover would win out. Oh, and we were trying to do this all while running a business, flying around the world to deliver keynotes and workshops, tending to our personal lives, and living continents apart. (Did we mention we enjoy a challenge?)

With this as a backdrop, it's clear there were plenty of opportunities for the project to create friction in our partnership, and had we not been paying attention, it likely would have. However, leaning into the five embodiments as we worked together led to very different results.

MATT

Beginning on the journey of coauthoring this book, I came in with my ego blazing. I had strong ideas about what needed to be covered, the voice, the structure, and even what comma style to use (Oxford commas FTW!). Having my ideas and preferences challenged felt personal. Feedback was often unproductive because I was showing up to *win* rather than listen or understand. Unfortunately, this mindset inevitably introduced a fork in the road: Either I could write the book I had in mind (most likely alone), or I could help write the most impactful book possible. Only once I had this realization was I able to let my guard down and truly collaborate. And it was not thanks to me!

I remember that we had been working through the chapter on curiosity and were fleshing out care and authenticity. My definitions didn't fully mesh with Jean's ideas, but rather than getting into an argument about it, Jean showed up curious.

"No, sorry, I don't agree with that," I said.

But instead of doubling down and telling me why she was right and I was wrong, Jean asked, "Hmm. Can you tell me a little more about where the disconnect is for you? I feel like we're aligned, but there's obviously some resistance. I want to make sure I'm understanding what is missing for you."

Oh, shit! I thought to myself. *Jean is actually practicing this stuff right now. I have been so focused on writing about it that I haven't been living it! I need to step up and take my own advice.*

In that moment of clarity, I stepped back and apologized for how I'd been showing up, and we dug into the core difference (which was so minor that I couldn't even remember what it was when recounting this story).

As we continued building out and updating the manuscript, we took the opportunity to use the work to do the work. In other words, the writing process itself became an opportunity for us to push further on the path toward embodiment and reinforce our relationship as not just coauthors but business partners and friends. We focused on the impact of how we were showing up on calls. We began calling ourselves out when we could sense that we were becoming defensive or worked up around something. We looked out for one another's well-being, whether it was being up too early, staying up too late, or balancing the writing process while navigating personal challenges. As the work continued, we also found more effective language to work through difficult conversations, setting us up for easier conflict resolution beyond this project.

What began as a somewhat uncomfortable, awkward, or even downright contentious process at times shifted to an opportunity to reinforce our bond and produce even better work. This was only possible because we focused on showing up curiously, sharing authentically, deeply caring for one another, consistently expressing our gratitude for one another, and taking ownership of ourselves, our relationship, and our work.

Now, just because we have been leveraging the five embodiments to strengthen our relationship, does that mean that it's always easy? We wish! We still have moments where we show up tired, fearful, defensive, and so on. We're human beings. That's part of the gig. While we may not have known the full depth and breadth of the challenge we were taking on, we did know that we could lean on the strength of our relationship to weather even the toughest storm.

Even during conflict, neither of us ever questioned each other's motives. Even when one or both of us was worked up—when we debated whose sentence structure was the best choice to introduce a new section—we both trusted that the other wanted the best version of our book and that going to bat for their opinion was in service of the best possible version, not selfish gains. There was no fear that challenging moments or even critical conflict would hurt the foundation of our mutual respect and admiration. Our commitment to the five embodiments reinforces that we are in this together. It makes it easier to let go of winning in the moment, resulting in a more balanced relationship triangle, and we *all* end up winning.

Having a trusted partner who is doing the internal work while simultaneously supporting and cocreating the container for shared improvement provides the grounded confidence to wade into the uncertain waters of life and work with less apprehension. The hard conversations are not as hard. The big risks we face feel smaller. And we have someone in our corner encouraging us to do things that we know we should do but don't always want to.

This isn't to say that we have it all figured out—we're still on the path. But we know that even when we may not know the answers, we aren't in it alone. And there's power in that.

Feedback

While we feel more confident navigating hard conversations now, when we think back to earlier in our careers and leadership journeys, before we developed these skills, we both individually struggled to navigate hard conversations well. We've come to learn over the years that this is one of the most universal leadership challenges to tackle. Almost every single leader we have spoken to has echoed this experience. We regularly hear that feedback conversations are a serious challenge. Studies show a high percentage of managers are uncomfortable or avoid giving feedback whenever possible.[2, 3]

At a time when low employee engagement costs the global economy $9.6 trillion, transforming feedback can be a game-changer for your team. Gallup conducted studies with 14,774 participants across 2,354 teams and found that meaningful feedback substantially influences employee engagement. In fact, 80 percent of participants who report receiving meaningful feedback in the past week are fully engaged, compared to the global average of 21 percent.[4]

How do the embodiments transform challenging conversations into mutually beneficial experiences filled with opportunities for growth? Let's start with common barriers to effective, meaningful feedback conversations: defensiveness, fear, blame, clichés, exaggerations, emotional outbursts, interpersonal criticism (instead of behavior or task critiques), and vague HR jargon.

Think of a recent moment when you experienced any one or a combination of the feedback barriers above. Can you identify an embodiment that was missing from the conversation? For example, we've never heard feedback filled with generic clichés and vague HR jargon that felt authentic. Additionally, where blame, emotional outbursts, exaggerations, and their friends show up, there is inevitably an ownership vacuum. This is why each of those common barriers and painful moments of awkward feedback interactions can be prevented or improved in real time with the five embodiments.

Creating a container that supports meaningful feedback and avoids those barriers requires thoughtful preparation, established trust, and upfront effort (before the moment even arises). Whether it is a potential new hire, a colleague new to your team, or a long-time direct report with whom you'd like to foster better communication, you can transform your feedback experience and outcomes by building a strong relationship container for the conversation before it begins.

While there are countless ways to integrate the five embodiments into your feedback process, let's focus on key strategies to help you and your team members step into more meaningful, effective feedback conversations. We will highlight some specific spots where individual embodiments shine. Remember, even when an embodiment isn't highlighted in a specific section, it's still present and influencing the space. (For example, you can craft questions that are simultaneously authentic and curious.) The embodiments, in addition to your values, are not separate boxes to check or independent skills to reach but rather *tools* that become even stronger when combined. With that in mind, let's dive in.

BEFORE THE FEEDBACK CONVERSATION

The pathway to meaningful and effective feedback begins with understanding your own relationship with hard conversations. Engage your **curiosity** and reflect on moments when you received negative feedback and situations when you had to provide either negative or positive feedback. What feelings come up for you?

Are there any behaviors or patterns you default to? Self-awareness is essential to a successful conversation about cocreating the ideal container. Next, extend your curiosity to include the person who will be receiving your feedback.

A helpful way to begin is by communicating the intention of the session: to provide meaningful and actionable feedback that will foster growth and development. To do this, initiate a conversation aimed at understanding the person's needs and preferences ahead of time. Ask how they prefer to receive feedback, and dig in with questions such as

Generally, are you more comfortable accepting compliments or criticisms?

How do you like to receive acknowledgment or recognition for work well done?

When it comes time for me to deliver difficult feedback, do you have any tips for how to best navigate those conversations with you?

Kicking off the conversation with open-ended questions, following up with clarifying questions, and sharing your own experience with feedback has the power to illuminate and inform. Their responses and the discussion that follows will offer helpful insights, opportunities for connection, and better levels of understanding each other **authentically**.

Asking them for their preferences is a starting point, not an instruction manual. Once you know more about them, you can propose a couple of options for feedback that you think will be a good fit. For example, if they prefer a formal written report, and based on your experience and schedule you know that isn't a realistic expectation, ask clarifying questions. Seek to understand what they most need and want from feedback to propose a compromise.

You each need to be able to be yourselves to set feedback up for success, which means creating a space where you both show up self-aware, honest, and willing to be vulnerable. Insincerity from either of you, even with the best of intentions, will drive disconnection and damage trust. Trust is a fundamental prerequisite of the containers best equipped to handle hard conversations with grace. As the person providing feedback, you have power: By opening up first, you can encourage vulnerability.

If you have a moment when your relationship with feedback changed, share it. Or if you can imagine the type of leader and kind of conversation that would have helped you get the most out of feedback, tell them about it.

For example:

My outlook on feedback changed when I finally realized that my tendency for self-criticism was getting in the way of making a change. Every time I heard critiques from my manager, whose opinion I deeply respected, my shame went into overdrive, and I'd shut down. While I intellectually knew that feedback was a great opportunity for growth, I had to finally come to terms with the fact that I really only loved it in theory—not practice. With that in mind, we began to build a new format for our feedback conversations. We figured out that if she asked me what I thought went wrong first, I would often identify most of what she thought needed improvement without needing her to add on. Have you had any similar insights about your relationship with feedback?

Showing up curious and investing the time to get to know someone more deeply with the hope to better communicate with them in the future demonstrates **care**, and it's an ideal beginning for healthy feedback. Over time, throughout your working interactions, when you experience authentic appreciation—in big and small moments alike—let them know. Regularly taking the time to express **gratitude** for someone's work and how they show up not only strengthens their confidence in their role and value to the team but also lets them know you notice and appreciate their contributions.

Once you know their preferences and set expectations leveraging your experience and authentic leadership style, you are well on your way to future feedback success!

WHEN THE MOMENT ARRIVES TO DELIVER FEEDBACK

Start with clear expectations. A caring way to ensure psychological safety is to open by transparently addressing reasonable fears: Share the topic, explain what is at stake, and specify the scope of the feedback and the potential ramifications that come along with it. The difference in knowing upfront if your job and livelihood are on the line or if your professional development targets simply haven't been met changes the entire experience and the tone of the conversation. Showing up in service of their personal or professional development, in a way that makes it easy to feel your care and intention, helps the receiver also show up open and curious. A little gratitude goes a long way. Rather than leverage a shallow, nice statement because you want to soften the blow of a harsh critique, come prepared with honest wins or things they got right specific to the same scope of feedback.

In the moment, mutual respect, appreciation, and care that reflect the authentic relationship you have built over time all help to limit blame and defensiveness and empower **ownership**. Ensure that when you are holding them accountable, you have also acknowledged your contribution to the situation, if they had adequate autonomy, and what may be restricting their levels of responsibility. Speak to your perspective openly and honestly and ask them to fill in the gaps and challenge your takeaway or reasoning if they feel you've missed something. How you show up either models and reinforces ownership or sets the stage to avoid it. When you practice before you preach, they're more likely to feel safe enough to share their perspective and own their part.

Have clear takeaways, work together toward a solution or improvement that you both feel good about, and make a plan to hold each other to it. Circle back to curiosity, care, and gratitude before closing: Tell them what you've learned, express your forward-looking expectations and hopes, and share gratitude. Always make sure they have the space to add or share anything else they want. Keep cultivating the trust in your relationship with the five embodiments leading up to the next feedback conversation, and take a deep exhale, knowing it gets progressively easier, more meaningful, and notably more effective with time and practice.

QUICK TIPS

But what if you have a feedback conversation this afternoon?

Although it's preferable to enter tough conversations with the security of a trusting relationship, that's not always an option. Sometimes you need to give someone feedback before you've had time to put in the work. Fortunately, even without a strong existing connection already in place, you can leverage the five embodiments to make your next conversation effective and impactful! Here's a quick list of things to remember for such an occasion:

CURIOSITY. Curiosity is an act of humility. The goal isn't to be right; it's to find the best path forward.

- **Do:** Seek to understand, question what you may be missing, invite their perspective(s), and find out how you can support them in improving the situation.
- **Don't:** Speak down to or over someone. Coming in with your mind made up kills any opportunity for deeper understanding.

AUTHENTICITY. Authenticity is contagious, and it starts with you.

- **Do:** Speak openly, honestly, and in your voice. Embrace vulnerability, and invite them to do the same.
- **Don't:** Perform or show up in a way that is not true to you; this drives disconnection and shuts down honest dialogue.

CARE. Feeling cared for by the person giving you feedback shifts how receptive you are to what they have to say.

- **Do:** Relinquish self-interest. Spend time in service of their growth to show care in a way that is meaningful to them.
- **Don't:** Vent or seek to shame. Those things serve your ego, not them.

GRATITUDE. Feedback shouldn't just be about discussing what's going wrong. It's an opportunity to reinforce what's going right.

- **Do:** Express relevant and recent gratitude: Point to a specific impact their work has had on you.
- **Don't:** Share inauthentic or generic compliments; artificiality degrades trust.

OWNERSHIP. Ownership is a two-way street. Embrace it as much as you expect it from others.

- **Do:** Reflect honestly, admit mistakes, share your perspective, and invite their perspective. Evaluate your respective levels of accountability, autonomy, and responsibility on each topic.
- **Don't:** Be a hypocrite. One-way ownership breaks relationships.

Workplaces where feedback flourishes don't limit it directionally. After all, the value of feedback isn't dictated by the rank or title of the person giving it. Each of us can get better at asking for, giving, receiving, and applying feedback to our continual development. The intention you put in at the start creates an upward spiral that becomes easier to maintain as you practice. Feedback provides an opportunity to develop better communication skills, increase resilience, and strengthen your relationship. And as your relationship becomes stronger and more resilient and you communicate better, feedback conversations become less daunting and more productive. And so on, in an upward spiral of growth and progress.

As the catalyst of change toward building a human-focused

workplace, even the pushback you receive is an opportunity for healthy feedback conversations. When you show up curious, authentic, caring, grateful, and embrace ownership—while seeking the insights their perspectives can provide—you reinforce the power of human-focused leadership, help them feel heard, seen, and valued, and each become stronger for it.

Eventually, as the upward spiral becomes more self-sustaining, others will jump in to contribute. Then, one day, when someone says, "Wow, your team handled that issue so well!" or marvels at your cohesive culture, you'll realize that what once felt impossible has become your new normal.

The future of work isn't a distant vision—it's being built right now, in every conversation, every decision, and every act of leadership. Every workplace transformation starts with one leader deciding to show up differently. Be that leader.

A Worthy Challenge

We're at an inflection point. The chasm between what leadership delivers and what humanity needs is deep. Over the last half a century, we've glorified a style of executive management defined by generating massive profits and prioritizing shareholders over everything and called it leadership. We've rewarded self-first behaviors from those in power and incentivized hypercompetitive self-first cultures. While there is nothing inherently wrong with making money, being self-reliant, or having a competitive spirit, when we over-index to the point where needing or even considering others is seen as a sign of weakness, we undermine ourselves and erode the very foundation of a healthy, thriving culture. From the rapidly expanding wealth gap to the debilitating loneliness epidemic, it is clear the choices we make and how we lead teams, organizations, and nations have widespread ramifications.

It may seem obvious that relationships are foundational to our well-being and have an irreplaceable role in our lives. After all, we know that simply seeing someone we have a warm connection with decreases our cortisol levels. We know that strong, supportive relationships increase our resilience and diminish stress levels. We know it is the people who manage us that most significantly influence our engagement, productivity, and decisions to quit. And we know that isolation increases our risk of heart disease, dementia, depression, anxiety, and premature death. Put simply, we know the quality of our relationships influences the quality and longevity of our lives.

Yet, how many of us actually behave in a way that reflects this, especially at work?

It's time to reevaluate the notion of work-life balance.

Although we support the goal behind the work-life balance movement (preventing work from consuming too much of our lives), the problem is right there in the name: It puts work at odds with life. Work is a part of life, not the thing you do when you're not living. We have one life. Whether you're working, doing recreational activities, resting, or anything else throughout your day, it is all life. Rather than trying to compartmentalize your work life and your life-life, we want to create a world where you get to be your whole embodied self, regardless of where you are.

This is, in large part, why we wrote this book, and why our proposal is not some radical, out-there idea. It simply acknowledges a timeless human truth: We need one another. It's rooted in our biology. We are social animals that benefit far more from cooperation than constant competition. By honoring our human needs to feel seen, heard, and valued, we empower one another to be our best selves. When we focus on strengthening the connections between us, we unlock our individual and collective potential.

Doing so, however, demands that we rethink our work cultures so that they feel less at odds with *living*. In other words, we need to create workplaces that don't suck.

Imagine for a moment a workplace—and even a world—where you know that, regardless of good times or bad, stress or abundance, you and the people around you will default to curiosity, authenticity, care, gratitude, and ownership. A future where you regularly feel cared for in the minor moments, the huge wins, and the big setbacks on your team. A workplace where colleagues lean into hard conversations with authenticity and come out stronger as a result. Where ownership is a shared mindset, a framework to set you up for success, a measuring stick to evaluate progress, and a way to inform and guide any needed changes. A world where people regularly express gratitude and share how others impact them. A place where we individually and collectively are curious enough to get to know ourselves, one another, and the world over and over again. A world where we focus less on winning and being right and more on learning and growing.

This future, and its resulting workplaces, can only be created by *Human-Focused Leaders*. We can create a workplace where people don't dread Mondays. A culture where leaders are known for their empathy as much as their strategy. A future where work enriches life rather than depletes it. But these workplaces will require thoughtful design and intention to infuse connection at every turn. And only people who keep humans and relationships at the forefront are equipped to do it. We hope you'll take the learnings from this book and apply them throughout your life to improve the strength of your relationships, your organizational culture and performance, and ultimately, the quality of your life and the lives of the people around you.

The challenge before us is simple but profound: Redefine leadership, not as power over others, but as responsibility for others, and build workplaces where people don't just survive—they thrive. We each deserve to feel a sense of value and pride in ourselves and our work, and it's our job as leaders to catalyze that feeling in those around us. To do that, we need to shift how we show up—for ourselves, for our teams, for the future. Leadership was never about a title. So, no matter what yours might be, consider this your call to step up.

The world doesn't need more managers. It needs leaders who embody curiosity, authenticity, care, gratitude, and ownership.

Take the first step—no matter how small—and take it now.

The world needs better leaders.

The world needs *you*.

Notes

CHAPTER 1

1   Dr. Vivek Murthy, US surgeon general, United States Department of Health and Human Services, YouTube, https://www.youtube.com/watch?v=B8pa506BFk4.

2   Cigna Corporation, "The Loneliness Epidemic Persists: A Post-Pandemic Look at the State of Loneliness Among U.S. Adults," 2021; Liana DesHarnais Bruce et al., "Loneliness in the United States: A 2018 National Panel Survey of Demographic, Structural, Cognitive, and Behavioral Characteristics," *American Journal of Health Promotion* 33, no. 8 (2019): 1123–33; Bridget Shovestul et al., "Risk Factors for Loneliness: The High Relative Importance of Age Versus Other Factors," *PLOS One* 15 (2020), https://doi.org/10.1371/journal.pone.0229087.

3   Anastasia Shvedko et al., "Physical Activity Interventions for Treatment of Social Isolation, Loneliness or Low Social Support in Older Adults: A Systematic Review and Meta-Analysis of Randomised Controlled Trials," *Psychology of Sport and Exercise*, 34 (2018): 128–137, https://doi.org/10.1016/j.psychsport.2017.10.003.

4   KFF's State Health Facts. Data Source: Bureau of Health Workforce, Health Resources and Services Administration (HRSA), U.S. Department of Health & Human Services, Designated Health Professional Shortage Areas Statistics: Designated HPSA Quarterly Summary, as of December 31, 2024, available at https://data.hrsa.gov/topics/health-workforce/shortage-areas.

5   John A. Sturgeon and Alex J. Zautra, "Social Pain and Physical Pain: Shared Paths to Resilience," *Pain Management*, 6, no. 1 (2016): 63–74, https://doi.org/10.2217/pmt.15.56.

6   Dr. Vivek Murthy, *Our Epidemic of Loneliness and Isolation: The U.S. Surgeon General's Advisory on the Healing Effects of Social Connection and Community*, Office of the U.S. Surgeon General, 2023, https://www.hhs.gov/sites/default/files/surgeon-general-social-connection-advisory.pdf.

7   Dr. Robert Waldinger (current director of the Harvard Study of Adult Development), "The Secret to a Happy Life—Lessons from 8 Decades of Research," YouTube: TED, November 2022, 00:00:44, https://www.ted.com/talks/robert_waldinger_the_secret_to_a_happy_life_lessons_from_8_decades_of_research/transcript.

8   State of the Global Workplace: 2025 Report, Gallup, https://www.gallup.com/workplace/349484/state-of-the-global-workplace.aspx.

9   Ray Oldenburg, *The Great Good Place: Cafés, Coffee Shops, Bookstores, Bars, Hair Salons, and Other Hangouts at the Heart of a Community* (Berkshire, 2023), https://doi.org/10.2307/jj.9561417.

10 Jeff Wiltse, "Troubled Waters: The Racial History of Swimming in the United States," Review of *Contested Waters: A Social History of Swimming Pools in America, The Journal of Blacks in Higher Education* 55 (2007): 94–95, http://www.jstor.org/stable/25073669; "Racial History of American Swimming Pools," NPR, May 6, 2008, https://www.npr.org/transcripts/90213675; Ryan Carney, "Swimming Pool Statistics & Industry Insights (2025)," RenoSys, May 6, 2025, https://renosys.com/swimming-pool-statistics-industry-insights-2024/#:~:text=According%20to%20Jobera%2C%20the%20U.S.,31%20people%20in%20the%20country.

11 Robert D. Putnam, *Bowling Alone: The Collapse and Revival of American Community* (Simon & Schuster, 2000).

12 Robert D. Putnam, "Robert Putnam—'Join or Die' & Building Communities to Save Democracy | The Daily Show," *The Daily Show* interview with Jordan Kleeper, November 12, 2024, YouTube, 00:02:45, https://www.youtube.com/watch?v=FOP_G2eiLo0.

13 Jeffrey M. Jones, "U.S. Church Membership Falls Below Majority for First Time," Gallup, March 29, 2021, https://news.gallup.com/poll/341963/church-membership-falls-below-majority-first-time.aspx.

14 Jeffrey M. Jones, "Church Attendance Has Declined in Most U.S. Religious Groups," Gallup, March 25, 2024, https://news.gallup.com/poll/642548/church-attendance-declined-religious-groups.aspx.

15 A. Gemar, "Religion and Loneliness: Investigating Different Aspects of Religion and Dimensions of Loneliness," *Religions* 15, no. 4 (2024): 488, https://doi.org/10.3390/rel15040488.

16 Katherine Schaeffer and Carolina Aragão, "Key Facts About Moms in the U.S.," Pew Research Center, May 9, 2023, https://www.pewresearch.org/short-reads/2023/05/09/facts-about-u-s-mothers/.

17 Brené Brown and Esther Perel, "Esther Perel on New AI—Artificial Intimacy," *Unlocking Us*, March 20, 2024, produced by Vox Media, podcast, https://brenebrown.com/podcast/new-ai-artificial-intimacy/.

18 "The Harris Poll: Recession Watch and Workplace Behavior Snapshot," Justworks, July 13, 2023b, https://www.justworks.com/lp/harris- poll#harris-poll- concerns-around-job-security.

19 Beth Ann Mayer, "Study: Working Parents Work Longer Hours Than Non-Parents—Maybe They're Scared of Losing Their Jobs," *Parents*, March 27, 2023, https://www.parents.com/study-working-parents-work-longer-hours-than-non-parents-7371829.

20 Jessica Dickler, "62% of Americans Are Still Living Paycheck to Paycheck, Making It 'the Main Financial Lifestyle,' Report Finds," CNBC, October 31, 2023, https://www.cnbc.com/2023/10/31/62percent-of-americans-still-live-paycheck-to-paycheck-amid-inflation.html.

CHAPTER 2

1 According to the US Department of Labor and surveys from the Bureau of Labor Statistics, the average employee age and retirement age have increased by around six and a half years and nearly two years, respectively, in the last fifty years alone ("Employed Persons by Detailed Occupation and Age," U.S. Bureau of Labor Statistics, January 29, 2025, U.S. Bureau of Labor Statistics, https://www.bls.gov/cps/cpsaat11b.htm).

2 This quote by Dr. Adhanom Ghebreyesus is from a joint news release ("Devastatingly Pervasive: 1 in 3 Women Globally Experience Violence," WHO website, March 9, 2021, https://www.who.int/news/item/09-03-2021-devastatingly-pervasive-1-in-3-women-globally-experience-violence).

3   We found other statistics for this section on the NCADV website (https://ncadv.org/STATISTICS), notably a quote by the NCADV; M. C. Black et al., "The National Intimate Partner and Sexual Violence Survey: 2010 Summary Report," Atlanta: National Center for Injury Prevention and Control, Centers for Disease Control and Prevention, 2011.

4   Amy Edmondson, "Psychological Safety and Learning Behavior in Work Teams," *Administrative Science Quarterly* 44, no. 2 (1999): 350–383, https://doi.org/10.2307/2666999.

5   "State of the Global Workplace: 2025 Report," Gallup, https://www.gallup.com/workplace/349484/state-of-the-global-workplace.aspx.

6   "What Is Employee Engagement and How Do You Improve It?" Gallup, accessed May 1, 2025, https://www.gallup.com/workplace/285674/improve-employee-engagement-workplace.aspx.

7   Caroline Castrillon, "Why Your Bad Boss Could Literally Be Killing You," *Forbes*, July 21, 2019, https://www.forbes.com/sites/carolinecastrillon/2019/07/21/why-your-bad-boss-could-literally-be-killing-you/?sh=1408a5606f24.

CHAPTER 4

1   John C. Maxwell and Jim Dornan, *Becoming a Person of Influence: How to Positively Impact the Lives of Others* (HarperCollins, 2006).

2   Bradley P. Owens and David R. Hekman, "How Does Leader Humility Influence Team Performance? Exploring the Mechanisms of Contagion and Collective Promotion Focus," *Academy of Management Journal* 59, no. 3 (2016): 1088–1111, https://doi.org/10.5465/amj.2013.0660.

3   Rob Nielsen and Jennifer A. Marrone, "Humility: Our Current Understanding of the Construct and Its Role in Organizations," *International Journal of Management Reviews* 20, no. 4 (2018): 805–824, https://doi.org/10.1111/ijmr.12160.

4   Lisa Feldman Barrett, "You Aren't at the Mercy of Your Emotions—Your Brain Creates Them," YouTube: TED, December 2017, https://www.ted.com/talks/lisa_feldman_barrett_you_aren_t_at_the_mercy_of_your_emotions_your_brain_creates_them?language=en.

5   Lindsay C. Gibson, "Disentangling from Emotionally Immature People with Lindsay C. Gibson," December 27, 2023, in *We Can Do Hard Things*, produced by Apple Podcasts, 56:31, https://podcasts.apple.com/us/podcast/264-disentangling-from-emotionally-immature-people/id1564530722?i=1000637763210.

CHAPTER 5

1   Becky Kennedy, *Good Inside: A Guide to Becoming the Parent You Want to Be* (HarperCollins, 2022).

2   Brené Brown, *Dare to Lead: Brave Work. Tough Conversations. Whole Hearts* (Random House, 2018).

3   Brené Brown, *Braving the Wilderness: The Quest for True Belonging and the Courage to Stand Alone* (Random House, 2017).

4   Stephen Shedletzky, *Speak-Up Culture: When Leaders Truly Listen, People Step Up* (Page Two, 2023).

CHAPTER 6

1   James Clear, *Atomic Habits: An Easy and Proven Way to Build Good Habits and Break Bad Ones* (International) (Random House Business, 2020).

CHAPTER 7

1   "Human Workplace Index: The Price of Invisibility", Workhuman, September 5, 2024, https://www.workhuman.com/blog/human-workplace-index-the-price-of-invisibility/; "Working to Survive," O.C.Tanner, n.d., https://www.octanner.com/global-culture-report/2025-working-to-survive.

2   Tiffany A. Ito et al., "Negative Information Weighs More Heavily on the Brain: The Negativity Bias in Evaluative Categorizations," *Foundations in Social Neuroscience* (2002), doi:10.7551/mitpress/3077.003.0041.

3   Paul Rozin and Edward B. Royzman, "Negativity Bias, Negativity Dominance, and Contagion," *Personality and Social Psychology Review* 5, no. 4 (2001): 296–320, https://doi.org/10.1207/S15327957PSPR0504_2.

4   Prathik Kini et al., "The Effects of Gratitude Expression on Neural
     Activity," *NeuroImage* 128 (2016): 1–10, https://doi.org/10.1016/j.
     neuroimage.2015.12.040; Glenn R. Fox et al., "Neural Correlates of
     Gratitude," *Frontiers in Psychology* 6, no. 1491 (2015), https://doi.
     org/10.3389/fpsyg.2015.01491; Sunghyon Kyeong et al., "Effects of
     Gratitude Meditation on Neural Network Functional Connectivity and
     Brain-Heart Coupling," *Scientific Reports* 7, no. 1 (2017): 5058, https://doi.
     org/10.1038/s41598-017-05520-9.

5   Christina M. Karns et al., "The Cultivation of Pure Altruism via
     Gratitude: A Functional MRI Study of Change with Gratitude Practice,"
     Frontiers in Human Neuroscience (2017): 599, https://doi.org/10.3389/
     fnhum.2017.00599.

6   Philip C. Watkins et al., "Joy Is a Distinct Positive Emotion: Assessment of
     Joy and Relationship to Gratitude and Well-Being," *The Journal of Positive
     Psychology* 13, no. 5 (2017): 522–39, https://doi.org/10.1080/17439760.2
     017.1414298.

7   Ronald J. Burke et al., "Virtues, Work Satisfactions and Psychological
     Wellbeing Among Nurses," *International Journal of Workplace
     Health Management* 2, no. 3 (2009): 202–219, https://doi.
     org/10.1108/17538350910993403.

8   Ellie Lisitsa, "The Four Horsemen: Contempt," Gottman Institute blog, May
     13, 2013, https://www.gottman.com/blog/the-four-horsemen-contempt/.

9   If you'd like to read more about contempt, we recommend checking out the
     work of Drs. John and Julie Gottman, https://www.gottman.com/about/
     john-julie-gottman/.

CHAPTER 8

1   "Ownership," *Merriam-Webster*, https://www.merriam- webster.com/
     dictionary/ownership; "ownership," *Cambridge Dictionary*, n.d., https://
     dictionary.cambridge.org/dictionary/english/ownership.

2   Ronald Fischer and Diana Boer, "What Is More Important for National
     Well-Being: Money or Autonomy? A Meta-Analysis of Well-Being, Burnout,
     and Anxiety Across 63 Societies," *Journal of Personality and Social Psychology*
     101, no. 1 (2011): 164–184, https://doi.org/10.1037/a0023663.

CHAPTER 10

1   "Mental Health at Work: Managers and Money," UKG, n.d., https://www.
    ukg.com/resources/white-paper/mental-health-work-managers-and-money.

2   Lou Solomon "Two-Thirds of Managers Are Uncomfortable
    Communicating with Employees," *Harvard Business Review*, March 9, 2016,
    https://hbr.org/2016/03/two-thirds-of-managers-are-uncomfortable-
    communicating-with-employees; Jack Zenger and Joseph Folkman, "Why
    Do so Many Managers Avoid Giving Praise?" *Harvard Business Review*,
    May 2, 2017, https://hbr.org/2017/05/why-do-so-many-managers-avoid-
    giving-praise; "Why People Crave Feedback—and Why We're Afraid
    to Give It: Working Knowledge," Harvard Business School, August 5,
    2022, https://www.library.hbs.edu/working-knowledge/why-people-
    crave-feedback-and-why-were-afraid-to-give-it; Joseph Folkman, "Leaders
    Beware: How Feedback Preferences Shape Your Effectiveness," *Forbes*,
    October 4, 2023, https://www.forbes.com/sites/joefolkman/2023/10/03/
    leaders-beware-how-feedback-preferences-shape-your-effectiveness/.

3   Jack Zenger and Joseph Folkman, "Why Do so Many Managers
    Avoid Giving Praise?" *Harvard Business Review*, May 2, 2017,
    https://hbr.org/2017/05/why-do-so-many-managers-avoid-
    giving-praise; "Why People Crave Feedback—and Why We're
    Afraid to Give It: Working Knowledge," Harvard Business School,
    August 5, 2022, https://www.library.hbs.edu/working-knowledge/
    why-people-crave-feedback-and-why-were-afraid-to-give-it.

4   "A Great Manager's Most Important Habit," Gallup May 30, 2023, https://
    www.gallup.com/workplace/505370/great-manager-important-habit.aspx.

Acknowledgments

To our friends and colleagues who offered time and thoughtful insights gained through their own book-writing processes—Peter Docker, Ashleigh Riddle, Rich Diviney, and Stephen Shedletzky— your advice and support were invaluable in guiding us through our own journey.

Jean

Mom, thank you for *everything*. Kelsey, your unwavering friendship and belief in me means the world. Mary, thank you for letting me crash your mornings whenever I need a chat or want to giggle with your boys. Jay, for all the encouragement and always making me feel like I belong, I am deeply grateful. Jacqueline, your friendship and support have literally and figuratively saved me repeatedly. Thank you.

To the Octopy team and all the colleagues I've had the pleasure to work with and who are the reason I know this work matters. Especially: Gabby, for truly embodying people-first leadership, and Paul, for expanding my understanding of the human mind and being an unwavering champion for employee well-being and a delightful co-creator. To my CS team, for your support of me chasing this dream even when it meant leaving our team *os adoro*.

Matt

To my dad: Thanks for being my original example of a human-focused leader. Every day, I hope to be a little bit more like you.

To my partner, Kellie, my family, and my friends: thanks for your patience with me while I've been exhausted, frustrated, and stressed. I appreciate your support more than you know.

To my colleagues in leadership development, past and present—Kristen Hadeed, Heath Slawner, Laura Gallaher, David Mead, Jen Waldman, Jana Wilder, Lori Jackson, the Williams-i, and my compadres at TOC (Simon, Sharin, Aisha, Taylor, Pai, Molly), as well as the fantastic leaders I've met along this journey: thanks for opening my eyes to the possibilities of this work and pushing me to go further.

About the Authors

Jean Larkin is a human-focused leadership expert who helps people learn and think differently. Bringing over a decade of experience redefining leadership, she has led multinational, multilingual, and multicultural teams at every phase of growth. Having worked across continents—from Uruguay to the UK, Spain to South Africa—in diverse sectors from travel and hospitality to software and telecommunications, Jean has unique insights into what connects us.

A lifelong learner and skilled teacher with extensive experience in course and program design, she thrives creating and delivering custom solutions that transform teams. Jean brings a multidimensional and adaptable perspective to whatever project she tackles. An early adopter of remote work and distributed teaming, Jean is an advocate of people-first policies.

Born in New York and a Spanish resident, Jean calls Mallorca home. The youngest of a large family, she describes herself as "a competitive ambitious geek" and a "recovering perfectionist." Outside of work, you'll find her practicing yoga, experimenting in the kitchen, creating art, or traveling to visit her favorite tiny humans (they call her aunt Jean).

Matt Dunsmoor has spent over a decade at the forefront of leadership development and organizational design, partnering with celebrated authors and global companies to build more human-focused workplaces. From coaching individuals to speaking on stages in front of thousands, Matt brings clarity, insight, and connection to every room.

He's worked with leaders in more than forty countries across six continents—from small start-ups to Fortune 100 giants—all with a common mission: making work suck less and helping people thrive.

Matt was born and raised in Colorado, though as a seasoned world traveler similar to his co-author, he feels at home wherever there is great coffee and even better conversations. A lifelong learner, he devours books, podcasts, TED Talks, and anything that explores leadership, philosophy, and the human experience.

When he's not on stage, writing, or reading, you'll likely find him playing basketball or volleyball, looking for ways to make friends and family laugh, or embracing his favorite role—proud uncle.

Matt and Jean co-founded Octopy to help organizations bring a more human focus to their organizational design and talent development. If you're interested in developing human-focused leaders, implementing *The Five Embodiments* with your team, or making sure your workplace doesn't suck, reach out to team@octopy.io! They'd love to hear from you.